Author's Note

The list of names covered in this book is by no means an exhaustive or comprehensive list of all the names used in Scotland or of Scottish origin, but is intended to be an alphabetical compendium of the most popular, influential, and interesting ones.

In many cases a definitive explanation for the meaning of the name has been lost in time. Often a name can have more than one meaning and certainly have more than one spelling. The definitions and spellings given in this book are the ones generally considered to be the most likely and commonly accepted. Wherever possible I have mentioned alternative suggestions as to the meanings of names.

The subject of Scottish names and their influence on the history of Scotland and the rest of the English-speaking world is a truly fascinating one. I would recommend that anyone who enjoys this book pursues further reading and research to gain a greater understanding of the people of Scotland.

There is a well-known Scottish phrase that we are all 'Jock Tamson's bairns', meaning that we are all the same under the skin. But this book shows that if the Scots want to seek a national identity then they have a unique and continually evolving heritage from which to source.

Editorial Staff
Ian Brookes
Helen Hucker

For the Publishers
Lucy Cooper
Elaine Higgleton

Collins
SCOTTISH
NAMES

HarperCollins Publishers
Westerhill Road
Bishopbriggs
Glasgow
G64 2QT

www.collinslanguage.com

First Edition 2009

ISBN 978-0-00-729946-1

Text © John Abernethy 2009

Illustrations © Alex Collier 2009

The moral rights of the author
have been asserted

The moral rights of the illustrator
have been asserted

Collins® is a registered trademark
of HarperCollins Publishers
Limited

A catalogue record for this book is
available from the British Library.

Designed and typeset by
Thomas Calla

Printed in Great
Clays Ltd, St I

Introduction

The history of Scotland is a remarkable story of invasions, battles, religion, industry, language, drink, and weather that could best be described as variable. A story of an ancient nation forged from Picts, Scots, Britons, Angles, and Norsemen whose language, cultures, and traditions had their origins in Ireland, England, Germany, and Scandinavia, amongst other places. All of these came together to create a country that the Romans called 'Caledonia', the Gaels called 'Alba', the Scots called 'Scotland' and the rest of the world thinks is somewhere in England.

The history of Scotland is, of course, the history of the Scottish people. And what could be more important as an indicator of how these Scots are perceived than the very names by which they are known. Moreover, over the centuries millions of Scots have left their homeland to find fame and fortune around the globe, and they have taken their Scottish names with them, so giving the world McDonalds and the Big Mac, Campbell's Tomato Soup, and Ross from *Friends*.

For many years, as in England, John Smith was the most common name in Scotland, but there is a huge variety and rich history of Scottish first names and surnames. Some of these are unique to Scotland or particularly associated with Scotland, and in the last fifty years more and more Scots have rejected English names and chosen traditional (and some not-so-traditional) Scottish names for their children.

The history of Scottish first names involves traditional Biblical names, names of saints, names of famous Scottish kings and queens, and names from the Highlands and Islands that became adopted throughout Scotland, either in their original Gaelic or translated into English.

Gaelic was the language of half of Scotland's people well into the 17th century and has given Scotland many of its most famous and popular first names. Today there may only be 50,000 speakers of what was once the national language (currently more people in Scotland speak Polish than Gaelic), but there are many more than 50,000 people called Donald, Angus, Calum, Iain, Eilidh, Morven, and the numerous other examples from the Gaelic tradition.

The history of Scottish surnames is, by comparison, a more recent thing. Until the 12th century most Scots did not have surnames. It was not until King David I's decision to give large amounts of Scottish land to Norman nobles in return for their support of the Crown that the Norman tradition of surnames came into fashion.

Choosing a surname was a somewhat haphazard

affair. You could be the son of somebody (Robertson, Davidson, Johnston) or adopt the Gaelic variation of 'Mac' rather than 'son' (MacDonald, MacLeod, MacKenzie). You could take your surname from the nobles who owned the land you worked on, or from the dominant chieftain in your area. You could be called after your occupation (Shearer, Smith, Taylor) or perhaps after a colour (Brown, Black, Gray). For example, Reid, the Scots word for 'red', is a popular Scottish surname, which is no doubt indicative of Scotland having a higher-than-normal percentage of gingers.

In the Highlands and Borders of Scotland, the clan system established dominant families, with tartans, mottoes, gatherings, and weddings, giving centuries of business to grateful kilt-makers. Scotland also became used to first names becoming surnames and surnames becoming first names (Scott, Ross, Gordon, Graham), as well first names and surnames being very similar (Robert Robertson, Andrew Anderson, Donald MacDonald).

Finally, Scotland has a long tradition of place names becoming first names or surnames (Murray, Angus, Hamilton). Even the name 'Scott' itself simply means 'someone who comes from Scotland'. In recent years the trend for naming children after Scottish place names has increased. Lewis is currently the most popular boys' name in Scotland, with Kyle also in the top ten, while some of Scotland's most popular girls' names are Isla, Skye, and Iona. So while it is unlikely that Scotland's top surnames will see many changes (although one wonders if a few Browns or Camerons might be keeping their surname quiet), Scottish first names are likely to see many new and surprising additions over the coming years – although whether Grangemouth or Cumbernauld will ever become popular remains debatable.

Abercrombie

Scottish surname that derives from the village of Abercrombie in Fife, meaning 'at the mouth of the River Crombie'. Famous Abercrombies includes American David T. Abercrombie who in 1892 founded what would become known as 'Abercrombie & Fitch', originally an outdoor-clothing company, and now one America's biggest retail brands.

Agnes

Female first name that was very popular in Scotland until comparatively recently. The name comes from the Greek and means 'pure' or 'chaste'. Saint Agnes of Rome was an early Christian virgin martyr. In Scotland the name became associated with Black Agnes, the 14th-century Countess of Moray, who successfully defended Dunbar Castle against the English. Diminutives of Agnes include Aggie, Nan, Nancy, Nessie (also an affectionate name of the Loch Ness Monster), and Senga (which is Agnes spelt backwards).

Aileen

Female first name that is an anglicized form of the Gaelic name Eilidh. Aileen is also a Scots variation of Eileen, the anglicized variation of the Irish name

Eibhlin, which came from the French *Aveline*, which in turn originated from the Germanic *Ava*. The original meaning is uncertain, but might possibly mean 'bird'. It is also possible that both Eileen and Aileen derive from the name Helen.

Ailsa

Female first name that derives from the island of Ailsa Craig in the Firth of Clyde. The island is uninhabited, other than by a large population of sea birds, and its name could possibly mean 'Elizabeth's rock' (from the Gaelic *Craig Ealasaid*), 'fairy rock' (from the Gaelic word *aillse*), or 'the island of Ael' (from the Norse *Aeley*). It could also derive from the name Elsa.

Ailsa Craig is colloquially known as 'Paddy's milestone' as it is halfway between Glasgow and Belfast.

Ainsley

Male first name that originated chiefly in the Borders. Ainsley comes from the surname Ainslie, which is found in both Scotland and England and originated from a place in Warwickshire called Ansley. Famous Ainsleys include television chef Ainsley Harriott.

Aitken

Scottish surname that is the Scots version of the
English surname Atkins. Atkins itself is a diminutive
of the first name Adam, the first man in the Bible,
with Adam simply meaning 'man' in Hebrew.
Famous Aitkens include Canadian newspaper
proprietor Max Aitken, better known as Lord
Beaverbrook, Matt Aitken (one-third of 1980s
pop producers Stock, Aitken, and Waterman), and
disgraced politician Jonathan Aitken.

Alexander

Male first name and surname coming from the Greek
and meaning 'protector' or 'defender of men'. The
name is long associated with Scotland, which has had
three King Alexanders. The most famous of these
was Alexander III, who gained the Hebrides from
Norway in 1266 and whose sudden death in 1286
began the political turmoil which would lead to
Scotland's Wars of Independence with England.

Other famous Scottish Alexanders include inventor
of the telephone Alexander Graham Bell, inventor of
penicillin Alexander Fleming, football manager Alex
Ferguson, First Minister Alex Salmond, golfer Sandy
Lyle, and Labour politicians Wendy and Douglas
Alexander.

Diminutives of Alexander include Alec, Alex, Alick, Eck, Lex, Zander, and Sandy.

Alison, Allison, Alyson

Female first name and surname, first recorded in Scotland in the 12th century as a diminutive form of Alice. The name Alice means 'noble' and was a variation of the French name Adelaide, which was brought to Britain by the Normans, but originated in the Germanic name *Adalhaidis*.

The name Alison remained popular in Scotland when it had fallen out of fashion elsewhere, and became regarded as a characteristically Scottish first name. Variations of Alison include Allison and Alyson and diminutives include Ally and Allie. Famous Alisons include singers Alison Moyet and Alison Goldfrapp, while Allison McBeal was the name of the surprisingly successful 1990s lawyer *Ally McBeal*.

Allison can also be found in Scotland as a surname, although it is generally thought that in this context Allison does not mean 'son of Alice', but is an anglicized form of MacAlister and means 'son of Alexander'.

Alistair, Alasdair, Alister

Male first name. Alasdair is the Gaelic form of Alexander, and Alistair is the anglicized form of

Alasdair. Popular diminutives of the name include Ally.

Famous Alistairs include broadcaster Alistair Cooke, who presented *Letter from America* on BBC Radio for 58 years, Chancellor of the Exchequer Alistair Darling, thriller writer Alistair Maclean, Scottish film actor Alistair Sim, occultist and 'wickedest man in the world' Aleister Crowley, footballer Ally McCoist, and manager of Scotland's disastrous 1978 World Cup campaign Ally MacLeod, who was celebrated somewhat optimistically in the song 'Ally's Tartan Army'.

Allan

Surname and male first name. Allan was initially found in north-east Scotland and is a variation of the first name Alan and the surname Allen, which are both common in England. The name Alan was brought to Britain by the Normans and originated from the French *Alain*. The origin of the name is unclear, with suggested meanings including the Breton for either 'rock' or 'handsome'. The Gaelic word for Allan is *Ailinn*, and this also means 'rock'. Famous Allans include Scottish Olympic sprint champion Allan Wells, Australian cricket captain Allan Border, and American writer of the macabre Edgar Allan Poe (whose adopted father was Scottish).

The town of Bridge of Allan is near Stirling and lies on the Allan Water (which also gives its name to the valley of Strathallan). In this case Allan is believed to have a different meaning from the personal name, possibly deriving from the Gaelic *aluinn* meaning 'sparkling' or from an older Brythonic word *alan* meaning 'swift'.

The Scottish surname MacAllan means 'son of Allan', and famous Macallans include the Macallan single malt whisky from Speyside.

Anderson

Surname that means 'the son of Andrew'. Anderson has long been considered a particularly Scottish surname, and is currently the eighth most common surname in the country. Famous Andersons of Scottish descent include television presenter Clive Anderson and *X Files* star Gillian Anderson. However, the family of Pamela Anderson, Canadian actress and probably the slowest runner in the world, comes from Finland.

Andrew

Biblical male first name meaning 'brave' or 'virile'. Andrew is associated with Scotland through Saint Andrew, who is the patron saint of Scotland (as well as of Russia and Greece). Andrew was one of Jesus' disciples, the brother of Saint Peter, and was crucified on a diagonal cross. Legend has it that his bones were brought to Scotland from Constantinople at some time between the 6th and 8th century and were buried in Fife in a location that would become the town of St Andrews. This town would become a major Scottish religious centre, and the now-ruined 12th-century St Andrew's Cathedral was for many centuries the largest building in Scotland. The Scottish flag or 'saltire' is based on the diagonal cross on which Saint Andrew died, and his feast day of November 30th has become the national day of Scotland.

Diminutives of Andrew include Andy and Drew, and famous Scottish Andrews include businessman and philanthropist Andrew Carnegie and tennis player Andy Murray.

The town of St Andrews would later find fame as the site of the first and arguably the most prestigious university in Scotland (founded in 1411) and later as the home of the Royal and Ancient Golf Club of St Andrews, the most famous golf course in the world and host of the Open Golf Championship on a record 28 times. Thus it is that the tradition, begun in the 9th century, of pilgrims from near and far travelling to St Andrews is continued, although now they bring their golf clubs and caddies with them.

Angus, Aonghus

Surname and male first name. The name comes from the Pictish and Gaelic name *Aonghus* or *Oengus* meaning 'unique choice' or 'one strength', which is associated both with a famous 8th-century Pictish King Oengus and the Celtic god Aengus Og.

The area of Scotland called Angus, which was one of the original minor kingdoms or mormaerdoms of Scotland and is now a local-government authority, is said to take its name from King Oengus.

Famous people called Angus include guitarist Angus Young from Australian rock band AC/DC (who was actually born in Glasgow) and television presenter Angus Deayton. *Angus, Thongs and Full-Frontal Snogging* is the name of a best-selling children's novel by Louise Rennison.

Diminutives of Angus include Gus and Gussie.

Ann, Anne

Female first name that has been one of the most popular names in Scotland (along with the rest of the English-speaking world) for centuries. The name derives from the Hebrew name Hannah, which features in the Bible as the name of the mother of Samuel and means 'favoured' or 'grace'. Queen Anne was the name of the last Stewart monarch of England and Scotland, and also the last monarch of Scotland before the Act of Union of 1707 (although Anne never set foot in her northern kingdom).

Diminutives of Anne include Nan and Annie, and famous Scottish Annes include singer Annie Lennox.

Archie, Archibald

Male first name. Archie became popular as a diminutive of the Scottish first name and surname Archibald. The name was brought to Scotland by the Normans and is Germanic in origin, meaning either 'bright gold' or 'noble and bold'. In Scotland, the name became associated with monks due to a misunderstanding between 'bold' and 'bald'.

Famous Archies include footballer Archie Gemmill, who scored perhaps the greatest goal in Scottish football history against the Netherlands at the 1978 World Cup – although of course Scotland still did not get through to the next round – and Archie Leach, which was the real name of film star Cary Grant.

Armour

Surname that derives from the occupation of armour-maker. Famous Scottish Armours include Jean Armour, long-suffering wife of Robert Burns, who would have nine children with Scotland's national bard, although it would not be until she had given birth to five of them that Burns got around to marrying her.

Armstrong

Surname from the Scottish-English Border region. The name is derived from the Old English words *earm* meaning 'arm' and *strang* meaning 'strong'. The founder of the Armstrongs was said to be a strong man who carried the king's armour. The Armstrongs lived up to their name by becoming one of the most powerful of the Border clans, known for their cross-border raiding. Famous Armstrongs with Scottish connections include astronaut Neil Armstrong, thus making the first person to set foot on the moon a Borderer.

Arran

Male first name. Arran is either a variation of the Biblical name Aaron, or has been inspired by the Scottish island of Arran, so continuing a trend that has seen other islands such as Lewis, Harris, Skye, and Iona become popular first names. The island of Arran takes its name from either the Gaelic *Arainn* or Brythonic *Aran* both of which means 'place of high peaks'.

Baillie

Scottish surname. The name derives from the Scots word *bailie*, which originates from the French *baillier* or English word 'bailiff', meaning someone who held the position of a magistrate or a senior member of a town or city council. The English surname Bailey has the same origin, although English bailiffs had different responsibilities.

Bain

Scottish surname (with the variation McBain) that originated in the north-east and derives from the Gaelic word *ban* meaning 'white' or 'fair'. Famous Bains and McBains include short-lived 11th-century Scottish king Donald Bain or Donald III, Shetland fiddler Aly Bain, and American crime writer Ed McBain (with McBain being the pen-name of the not very Scottish Salvatore Lombino).

Baird

Scottish surname that originates from the Gaelic word *bard* meaning 'bard' or 'minstrel' and became prominent in Ayrshire. Famous Bairds include Scottish inventor of television John Logie Baird, because of whom many bards and minstrels have gained audiences of millions.

Balfour

Scottish surname that originated from a place name in Fife that possibly means 'place of pasture' in Gaelic.

Scottish politician Arthur Balfour served as British Prime Minister between 1902 and 1905 and as Foreign Secretary in 1917 wrote the 'Balfour Declaration', which became famous for stating Britain's official support for a Jewish state. Another famous Scottish Balfour was engineer George Balfour, who in 1909 co-founded Balfour Beatty, currently one of the largest construction companies in the world.

Ballantine, Ballantyne, Bannatyne

Scottish surname with various different spellings originating from different place names in the Borders and Lanarkshire. The meaning of Ballantine and

Bannatyne is uncertain, with suggested meanings including 'place of the farm' (from the Gaelic). However, a Brythonic origin is also possible, with the Borders place name of Bellenden possibly meaning 'place of worship for Bel' (Bel being the Celtic god of light and fire).

Famous Ballantines include Scottish author of *Coral Island* R.M. Ballantyne and Ballantine's blended whisky from Dumbarton. Famous Bannatynes include businessman and the person least likely to offer any money on television's *Dragon's Den*, Duncan Bannatyne.

Barbour

Scottish surname that originates from the Scots word for the occupation of barber and is a Scottish variation of the English surname Barber. The Barbour waterproof jacket is made by the firm of J. Barbour & Sons, which was founded in Galloway in 1894.

Barclay

Surname and occasional male first name that originated from a Norman family called de Berkeley and the Gloucestershire village of Berkeley. The Scottish form of the surname became prominent in Aberdeenshire and it was Montrose banker James

Barclay who in 1736 gave his name to Barclay's Bank, one of twenty largest companies in the world and (at the time of writing) the third-largest bank in the United Kingdom.

Barr, Barrie

Surnames that derive from the Gaelic word *barr* meaning 'hilltop', which is found in several Scottish place names. Famous Barrs include American comedienne Roseanne Barr (whose family were East European Jews who changed their name to Barr) and Scottish soft drinks company A. G. Barr & Co, best known for producing Scotland's other national drink 'Irn Bru', said to have girders as one of its ingredients.

The surname Barrie derives from Barr and originated in Angus. Famous Barries include Scottish author of *Peter Pan* J.M. Barrie. Barrie is also the name of a Canadian town in Ontario named after a British naval officer with Scottish origins called Robert Barrie.

Baxter

Surname that is a Scots form of the occupation of baker and is thought to have originally referred to a female baker. Famous Baxters include *Tomorrow's World* presenter Raymond Baxter, Scottish comedian

Stanley Baxter, Scottish footballer Jim Baxter, and the Scottish firm of Baxter's from Fochabers where, continuing the tradition of the name's origin, it was Ethel Baxter who invented the recipe for Royal Game Soup.

Beaton

Surname that originated in the Lowlands from a Norman surname Bethune, which came from a place name in Northern France also called Bethune. The place name is of uncertain origin, but is possibly derived from a personal name 'Betto'. In the Highlands, Beaton is also the anglicized form of the surname MacBeth, meaning 'son of life'. The Beaton family were prominent in the 16th century as Scottish archbishops and chancellors, and other famous Beatons include costume designer Cecil Beaton.

Beattie, Beatty

Surname that either originates from the Gaelic word *biadhtaich* meaning the occupation of 'victualler' or 'food supplier', or from a diminutive of the male first name Bartholomew. Bartholomew was one of Jesus' disciples, whose name is believed to be the Aramaic for 'son of Talmai', with *Talmai* being a Hebrew first name. Famous Beattys include American actors

Warren Beatty (Shirley MacLaine's brother) and Ned Beatty, who probably never bought or supplied bacon again after starring in *Deliverance*.

Bell

Surname that is popular throughout Britain. The name derives either from the occupation of bell-ringing or bell-making, or from the French world *bel* meaning 'handsome', or in Scotland as an anglicized form of Macmillan – in Argyll the Macmillans were known as *Clan na Belich*. Famous Scottish Bells include inventor of the telephone Alexander Graham Bell, builder of *The Comet*, the first passenger steamer in Europe, Henry Bell, and 'Bell's' from Perth, one of Scotland's most popular blended whiskies.

Birss

Scottish surname that comes from a place name in Aberdeenshire. The place name comes from the Gaelic word *birss* meaning 'bush'.

Black

Popular surname throughout Britain meaning 'black' or 'black-haired'. In Scotland the surname Black was often chosen by MacGregors and members of other Highland clans in the period when their clan names were banned. Famous Scottish Blacks include scientists Joseph Black, who pioneered the study of gases, and James Black, who won the Nobel Prize for Medicine in 1988.

Blair

Surname and male first name that is derived from the Gaelic place name *Blar* for 'cleared level land' or 'place of the battlefield'. Blair is first recorded as a surname in the 13th century in Renfrew and Ayrshire. Famous Blairs include author of *1984* and *Animal Farm* George Orwell (whose real name was Eric Blair), star of *The Exorcist* Linda Blair, and Edinburgh-born former British Prime Minister Tony Blair. The name is also famous from the cult 1999 horror film *The Blair Witch Project*, which – despite its name – did not feature the then Prime Minister or any of his family.

There are many Scottish places that have Blair as part of their name, such as Blairgowrie, Blair Atholl, and Blair Drummond Safari Park. Blair Castle, near Blair Atholl in Perthshire, is the seat of the Duke of Atholl.

Bonnie

Female first name that derives from the Scots word *bonnie* or *bonny* meaning 'pretty' (as in the famous song-line 'On the bonny, bonny banks of Loch Lomond').

The name became popular as a first name in the 1930s through the character of Bonnie Butler, daughter of Rhett and Scarlett, in the book and film *Gone with the Wind*, and infamous outlaw Bonnie Parker, who would be the subject of the 1967 film *Bonnie and Clyde* (perhaps it was their Scottish names that brought them together). Other famous Bonnies around the world have included country singers Bonnie Raitt and Bonnie Tyler, but in Scotland the name is really only popular as a name to give your dog.

Boswell

Scottish surname of Norman origin. The name derives from the French *bois* meaning 'wood' and *ville* meaning 'town', or perhaps from a French place name Beuzeville. However, in the case of the Borders place name St Boswell's the name derives from the 7th-century Saint Boisil. Famous Boswells include James Boswell, the Scottish biographer and companion of Dr Samuel Johnson. Newton St Boswell's is the administrative centre of the Scottish Borders.

Bowie

Surname that comes from the Gaelic *buidhe* meaning 'yellow-haired'. Famous Bowies include Jim Bowie, the American soldier who died at the Alamo and gave his name to the Bowie knife (a large hunting knife with which he was proficient), and iconic singer David Bowie, who was born David Jones but took Bowie as his stage name. Among the numerous different hair colours that Bowie would have over his career, yellow and peroxide would certainly feature quite prominently.

Boyd

Scottish surname and occasional male first name that originated in Ayrshire and Bute. The name comes from the Gaelic *buidhe* meaning 'yellow-haired'. Famous Boyds include Scottish hobbit Billy Boyd and Woody Boyd, the character in *Cheers* played by Woody Harrelson.

Boyle

Surname that in Ireland derives from O'Boyle (where it possibly means 'pledge'), but in Scotland also originates from the de Beauville family. The de Beauvilles came from the town Beauville in Normandy, and became established in Galloway in the 12th century. Famous Scottish Boyles include author Jimmy Boyle and comedian Frankie Boyle.

Bremner

Scottish surname that derives from the surname Brebner. The Brebners were originally people from the Brabant area of what is now Belgium and the southern Netherlands. Famous Scottish Bremners include footballer Billy Bremner, impressionist Rory Bremner, and actor Ewen Bremner, best known as Spud from *Trainspotting*.

Brenda

Female first name. Although in Ireland the name has been used as a female equivalent of Brendan, it is thought to be originally Scottish, possibly originating in Shetland and deriving from the Norse *brand* meaning 'sword'. It became a popular name after a character in Sir Walter Scott's 1822 novel *The Pirate*, which was set in the Northern Isles. Famous Brendas include American singer Brenda Lee and English actress Brenda Blethyn.

Brodie

Scottish surname that originated from the place name Brodie in Moray. The name of the place is derived from the Gaelic *brothaich* meaning 'muddy place'. Famous Brodies include Deacon William Brodie, 18th-century Edinburgh councillor by day and burglar by night, and the inspiration for *Dr Jekyll and Mr Hyde*, and Miss Jean Brodie, the fictional Edinburgh teacher of the 'crème de la crème' in the novel and film *The Prime of Miss Jean Brodie*.

Brown

Second most common surname in Scotland. Brown is an English word, coming from the French *brun* meaning 'brown-haired'. The Scottish nickname for Brown is Broon. Famous Scottish Browns include Queen Victoria's servant John Brown, Orcadian writer George Mackay Brown, and Scotland's most popular cartoon family *The Broons*, consisting of Grandpaw Broon, Maw Broon, Paw Broon, Joe Broon, Hen Broon, Maggie Broon, Daphne Broon, Horace Broon, the twins, and the bairn. Then of course there is Prime Minister Gordon Brown. The phrase 'browned off' meaning 'to be disappointed' was not actually coined in reference to the current Prime Minister.

Bruce

Scottish male first name and surname. The name Bruce comes from the Norman family Brus (or

Bruis), who came to Scotland and were given land at Annandale in the 12th century by David I. The Annandale de Brus family would first become the Earls of Carrick and finally the Scottish royal family of Bruce through the deeds of Robert I or Robert the Bruce, Scotland's most famous king who defeated the English at the Battle of Bannockburn in 1314. The name is believed to originate from the Norman place name of Brix, meaning 'willowlands', although this has been disputed.

Famous people called Bruce include martial-arts star Bruce Lee, perennial television star Bruce Forsyth, American film star Bruce Willis, and American singer Bruce Springsteen.

The Bruce Highway in Australia is the name of the Queensland coastal road that runs from the state capital Brisbane to Cairns in Far North Queensland and is nearly 1700 kilometres long. Bruce became a very popular name in Australia, leading to the misconception that it was compulsory for all Australian males to have this as their first name.

Bryce, Bryson

Surnames that have a common Scottish origin. Bryce is a surname that is also used as a male and female first name. It originated as a Scottish form of the male personal name *Brice*, derived from the

5th-century French Saint Bricius, whose name in turn possibly derived from a Welsh first name *Brych* meaning 'speckled'. The surname Bryson means 'son of Bryce'. Famous Bryces include American film actress Bryce Dallas Howard. Famous Brysons include American travel writer Bill Bryson.

Buchanan

Scottish surname that derives from the Buchanan district on the eastern shore of Loch Lomond. The name is Gaelic and means 'priest's house'. Famous Buchanans include 19th-century American President James Buchanan, husband and wife Tom and Daisy Buchanan from *The Great Gatsby*, Scottish world boxing champion Ken Buchanan, and Keisha Buchanan of pop group The Sugababes. Buchanan Street and the Buchanan Galleries are at the very heart of Glasgow's city centre and are named after Glaswegian tobacco lord Andrew Buchanan.

Burnett

Surname that originated in Aberdeenshire. The name comes from a family by the name of Burnard who were given land there in the 14th century. The meaning of that name is uncertain, but it has been suggested that it either derives from the French word *burnete* meaning 'brown' or from the male first name

Bernard. Bernard is of Germanic origin and was brought to Britain by the Normans. It means 'brave bear'.

Famous Burnetts include author Frances Hodgson Burnett, who wrote *The Secret Garden* and *Little Lord Fauntleroy*.

Burns

Surname that is associated with arguably Scotland's most famous son, Robert Burns. The name is not exclusively Scottish and probably derives from the English word *burn* meaning 'stream'. The life of Robert Burns is celebrated annually on January 25th, Burns' birthday. In fact, this day is celebrated more than St Andrew's Day (both in Scotland and internationally) and is the unofficial national day of Scotland.

Busby

Surname that derives from a place name found in both England and Scotland. The place name comes from the Norse *busk-by* and means 'bushy place'. There is a place called Busby in East Renfrewshire that has become a suburb of Glasgow. Famous Scottish people called Busby include football manager Matt Busby. His young Manchester

United team of the 1950s was known as 'The Busby Babes' and had already won the English league championship three times before many of their number died in the 1958 Munich air crash.

Cairns

Scottish surname and occasional male first name. The name derives from the Gaelic word *cairn* that has transferred into the English language as 'a pile of stones used to mark a boundary or a memorial'. William Wellington Cairns was the 19th-century Governor of Queensland in Australia after whom the city of Cairns in northern Queensland was named in 1876. Cairns has become a very popular holiday destination, offering access to the Great Barrier Reef, although the original Scottish pronunciation has been changed to the more Australian 'cans'.

Calder

Surname that in Scotland has several origins. In the Lowlands, Calder originates from the place name that is found in the West Lothian towns of West Calder, Mid Calder and East Calder. It is believed to derive from the Brythonic *caled dobhar* meaning 'rough water'. Famous Calders include American sculptor Alexander Calder, who is credited with inventing the children's mobile in 1931, and British Lions rugby captain Finlay Calder, who was first picked to play for Scotland in 1986, much to the delight of all his family – except for his twin brother Jim Calder, whose place he took in the side.

Calum, Callum

Calum is currently the fifth most popular first name for Scottish boys. Calum is the Scottish form of the Irish *Colm* and of the Latin *Columba* and means 'dove'. Saint Columba (or *Colum Cille* in Gaelic) was the Irish missionary who settled on the island of Iona and helped to establish Christianity in Scotland. Until medieval times it was not considered appropriate to have the same name as such an important saint as Columba, and so the name Malcolm (which means 'follower of Saint Columba') was used. Calum is currently the most popular name of Gaelic origin for Scottish boys.

Cameron

Long-standing Scottish surname that is now a popular first name. Cameron is the sixth most popular boys' name in Scotland and is also increasingly popular as a name for girls. The name comes from the Gaelic *camsron* meaning 'crooked nose' or 'hooked nose', so the Camerons have clearly not always been lookers. The Clan Cameron came

from the Lochaber area. Famous Camerons include director of *Titanic* James Cameron and film actress Cameron Diaz – probably one of the last people in the world you would expect to have 'hooknose' as a first name.

Cameron also appears to be a popular medical name. There are Dr Camerons in both *Doctor Finlay's Casebook* and the American hospital drama *House* – although they look somewhat different.

Another notable Cameron is possible future British Prime Minister (and possible last Prime Minister of the United Kingdom as we know it), Conservative leader David Cameron, who comes from a family of Scottish stockbrokers. His father was born near Huntly.

Campbell

Sixth most common surname in Scotland and occasional male first name. The name comes from the Gaelic *cambeul* meaning 'wry mouth' and the French *champ bel* meaning 'beautiful field'.

The Campbells became one of the dominant clans in Scotland with the clan chieftain gaining the title of Duke of Argyll in 1701. The family seat is at Inveraray Castle.

The Clan Campbell has been associated with Argyll

since at least the 13th century, but other Campbells became established in Breadalbane in Perthshire, Loudon in Ayrshire, and Cawdor in Moray. The Campbells were prominent supporters of first the Scottish and then the British Crown and supplied most of the men for the first Highland regiments in the British army. Colin Campbell was the Scottish soldier who led the 'Thin Red Line' in the Crimean War and took command of the British army in response to the Indian Mutiny of 1857.

Other famous Campbells include supermodel Naomi Campbell, country singer Glen Campbell, father and son world land and water speed record holders Malcolm and Donald Campbell, spin-doctor Alastair Campbell, actress Neve Campbell, UB40 singing brothers Ali and Robin Campbell (who come from a family of Scottish folk singers), and the Campbell's Soup Company. Famous Scottish Campbells include two Liberal leaders: Henry Campbell-Bannerman, who was British Prime Minister from 1905 to 1908, and more recently Menzies Campbell, who was not Henry's brother, in spite of jibes about his age.

The Campbell tartan is often called the 'Black Watch' and the majority of the original Black Watch or First Highland Regiment raised in 1725 were Campbells. The song 'The Campbells are Coming, Oho! Oho!' implied that they were not to be messed with.

Campbeltown is a town in Kintyre that was established by the Campbells and once proclaimed itself the word capital of whisky with over thirty distilleries. However, this number has sadly now been reduced to just three.

Cargill

Historic Scottish surname that originates from the place called Cargill in Perthshire. The name possibly derives from the Brythonic language and means 'white fort'. Cargill Inc. from Minnesota in the United States is one of the largest agricultural corporations in the world.

Carlyle

Surname that comes from the English city of Carlisle near to the Scottish border. The name is English in origin and it is not surprising that it should first have been found in Scotland just over the border in Dumfries and Galloway. Famous Scottish Carlyles include 19th-century historian Thomas Carlyle and actor Robert Carlyle.

Carmichael

Scottish surname that originated from the place in South Lanarkshire called Carmichael. The first part of the name is derived from the Brythonic *caer* meaning 'fort', and the second from the male first name Michael meaning 'who is like God'. Michael was an archangel in the Bible, and the name was brought to Britain through the French variation of *Michel*. Famous Carmichaels include English actor Ian Carmichael and American songwriter Hoagy Carmichael, who wrote 'Georgia on My Mind'.

Carnegie

Scottish surname that derives from a place name in Angus, The name is Gaelic and means 'the fort in the gap'. The most famous Scottish Carnegie is Andrew Carnegie from Dunfermline, who in the 19th century became one of the wealthiest men in America. He gave his name to numerous institutes, museums, and libraries around the world, as well as the world-famous musical venue Carnegie Hall in New York. There is another Carnegie Hall in his native Dunfermline, which is known throughout Fife.

Carson

Scottish surname of uncertain origin. The name could mean 'son of Carr (or Kerr)' but probably derives from an unknown Norman family name. The surname Carson was taken from Scotland to

Northern Ireland, and famous Ulster Carsons include Unionist politician Edward Carson and comedian Frank 'it's a cracker' Carson. Other famous Carsons include Scottish jockey Willie Carson, American chat-show host Johnny Carson, and American frontiersman Kit Carson, after whom the state capital of Nevada, Carson City, is named.

Catherine, Katherine

Popular female first name in Scotland for many centuries. The name is of Greek origin and associated with an early Christian martyr, Saint Catherine. The original meaning is unclear, but it is often taken to mean 'pure'. Diminutives of Catherine and Katherine include Cath, Cathy, Kate, Kathy, and Kitty.

Catriona

Female first name that is the Gaelic version of Catherine or Katherine and so means 'pure'. Famous Catrionas include Catriona MacGregor, the heroine of Robert Louis Stevenson's 1893 novel *Catriona*, which was the sequel to the more famous *Kidnapped*.

Chalmers

Scottish surname that derives from the Scots word *chalmer*, which is a variation of 'chamber'. Famous people called Chalmers include Thomas Chalmers, first moderator of the Free Church of Scotland (or Wee Frees) in 1843, Stevie Chalmers, scorer of the winning goal in Celtic's 1967 European Cup win, and Judith Chalmers, presenter of numerous television travel shows.

Charles

Male first name that derives from the Germanic name Karl. The original name means 'free man' and was translated into the French as Charles. It has been associated with royalty from the time of the Frankish Emperor Charlemagne ('Charles the Great'). Charles I of England and Scotland was born in 1600 in Dunfermline, the last Scottish-born monarch, and further Stewart Charleses were the merry monarch Charles II and Bonnie Prince Charlie himself, Charles Edward Stuart. Despite the disastrous end to the Jacobite Rebellion, Charles remained a popular first name in Scotland with famous Scottish holders of the name including architect and designer Charles Rennie Mackintosh and former Liberal Democrat leader Charles Kennedy.

Diminutives of Charles include Charlie and Chic. Charlie is now a popular boys' name in its own right, and 'Charlie Is My Darling' is a popular Jacobite song. The diminutive Chic is especially associated with Scottish comedian Chic Murray, who once said, 'I drew a gun, he drew a gun, I drew another gun, and soon we were surrounded by lovely drawings of guns.'

Chisholm

Scottish surname that became established in the Highlands but originated from a Norman family in the Borders. The Chisholm family took its name from a place in Roxburgh called Chesilholm, but later moved north to own land near Inverness. The original place name of Chesilholm is derived from the Old English *chesil* meaning 'gravel' and *holm* meaning 'island'. Famous Chisholms include singer Melanie Chisholm, better known as Mel C or Sporty Spice.

The American form of the name is Chisum, and *Chisum* was the name of a 1970 western in which John Wayne played the real-life cattle baron John Chisum.

Christie

Surname and first name for boys and girls. The name originates as a diminutive of the first names Christopher and Christian and became prominent in Fife. Famous Christies include the world's most popular crime writer Agatha Christie, film star Julie Christie, sprinter Linford Christie, and the London auctioneering firm of Christie's.

Clark, Clerk

Surname that has long been popular throughout Britain. The name comes from the occupation of clerk or scholar. Famous Scottish Clarks include world motor-racing champion Jim Clark and renowned scientist James Clerk Maxwell.

Cochrane

Scottish surname that originated from a place in Renfrewshire called Coveran. The origin of the place name is uncertain but possibly comes from the Brythonic *coch* meaning 'red'. Famous Cochranes include Scottish naval commander Thomas Cochrane, who at different times of his career led the navies of Chile, Brazil, and Greece, and American rock-and-roller Eddie Cochran, who died at the age of 21 and had a posthumous number-one hit with the prophetic 'Three Steps to Heaven'.

Colin

Male first name that has several origins. In Scotland Colin is often an anglicized form of the Gaelic

Cailean meaning 'young dog' or a variation of
the names Columba and Calum, meaning 'dove'.
Sometimes, as in England, it is a diminutive of the
first name Nicholas. Famous Scottish Colins include
soldier Colin Campbell, who led the British forces at
the time of the Indian Mutiny of 1857, golfer Colin
Montgomerie, and rally driver Colin McRae.

Collins

Surname that has several origins. The name is
predominantly an Irish surname from the Irish
O'Coleain meaning 'son of Coleain' (with *Coleain*
meaning 'young dog'), but it may also derive from
the first name Colin (whose various origins are
discussed on the preceding entry) and mean 'son of
Colin'.

Famous Scots called Collins include William Collins,
who founded the Glasgow publishing company that
would become internationally famous for bibles and
dictionaries and is now part of the HarperCollins
publishing group, and Edwyn Collins who first came
to fame as lead singer of the group Orange Juice.

Colquhoun

Scottish surname that comes from a place in
Dunbartonshire called Colquhoun. The name is

Gaelic and means 'narrow wood'. The surname is pronounced 'cohoon' with the 'l', 'q' and 'u' all silent. Perhaps understandably, the name has often been simplified to Calhoun and Cowan.

Corbett

Surname that came to Scotland from England. The name is derived from the French word *corbet* meaning 'raven'. Famous Scottish Corbetts include comedian Ronnie Corbett, who was the smaller of *The Two Ronnies*. The 219 peaks in Scotland that stand between 2500 and 3000 feet (and so are not quite high enough to be Munros) are known as Corbetts, after an English hillwalker called J. Rooke Corbett who compiled a list of them.

Craig

Male first name and surname that derives from the Gaelic world *creag* meaning 'rock'. The Craigs were people who lived next to a prominent crag or cliff. Famous Craigs include James Craig, the Scottish architect who designed Edinburgh's New Town, Daniel Craig, who is the current James Bond, and Wendy Craig, star of the classic television comedy series *Butterflies*.

Cranston

Surname that originated in the Borders and the
Lothians. The name is derived from *crane*, the bird,
and *ton* meaning 'town'. There is a city called Cranston
in Rhode Island in the United States, and famous
Scottish Cranstons include Kate Cranston, proprietor
of the famous Willow Tea Rooms in Glasgow.

Crawford

Surname and boys' first name. The name originates
from a village in Lanarkshire that derives from the
Scots word *craw* meaning 'crow' and the English
word *ford*. Famous Crawfords include the American
film star Joan Crawford, American model Cindy
Crawford, and actor Michael Crawford, star of *Some
Mothers Do 'Ave 'Em*.

Crichton

Scottish surname that takes its name from a place
in Midlothian. The place name is derived from the
Gaelic *crioch* meaning 'boundary' and the Scots word
ton meaning 'town' or 'village'. Famous Crichtons
include Michael Crichton, the author of *Jurassic Park*,
and the 16th-century Scot James Crichton, who
was famed for being an intellectual prodigy before
dying at the age of only 18, and inspired the J.M.

Barrie novel *The Admirable Crichton*. The name is pronounced 'cry-ton', with the 'ch' being silent.

Cumming, Comyn

Variations on the historic surnames Comyn and Cumin. The original surnames originated as Norman first names, or alternatively from an Old Celtic first name *Coman*. The Comyns were one of the most powerful families in Scotland in the 13th century, with lands in the Borders and Badenoch. John 'the Red' Comyn was prominent in resistance against the English occupation, but was killed by his rival Robert the Bruce in 1306, after which the family's influence went into decline. Famous Scots with the name Cumming include actor Alan Cumming.

Cunningham

Surname that originates from the Ayrshire district of Cunninghame. The place name may have its origins in the Gaelic word *cuinneag* meaning 'milk-pail'. Famous Cunninghams include the Cunningham family from American television series *Happy Days*.

Dalglish, Dalgleish, Dalgliesh

Scottish surname that comes from the Gaelic *dail* meaning 'field' and *glaise* meaning 'brook' or 'stream'.

The original spelling of the name was Dalgleish. The name is associated with one of Scotland's most famous sportsmen, Celtic and Liverpool footballer Kenny Dalglish. Adam Dalgleish was the name of the police commander in many of the crime novels of P.D. James.

Dalziel, Dalyell

Scottish surname that originates from a place called Dalzell in Lanarkshire. The place name derives from the Gaelic words *dail* meaning 'field' and *gheal* meaning 'white'. The letter 'z' is not traditionally pronounced in the surname Dalziel, and Dalyell has become a common variation. Famous Dalziels include brusque Yorkshire policeman Andy Dalziel, who features in the crime novels of Reginald Hill (and latterly the television series *Dalziel and Pascoe*), and Scottish politician Tam Dalyell, who famously asked the yet-to-be-answered 'West Lothian Question'.

David

Biblical male first name meaning 'beloved'. David has long been a popular name in Scotland, and there were two Scottish kings of that name. Common diminutives are Dave, Davie, and Davy. Famous Scottish Davids include philosopher David Hume, explorer David Livingstone, and *Doctor Who* actor David Tennant.

Davidson

Surname that means 'son of David' and is found throughout Britain (although is more associated with Scotland than England). The Davidsons are also a clan established in Speyside from the 13th century onwards, and famous Davidsons include comedian Jim Davidson and Arthur Davidson, co-founder of the Harley-Davidson motorcycle company.

Davina

Female first name that originated in Scotland. Davina is a feminine of David, and so means 'beloved'. Famous Davinas include television presenter Davina McCall, who is 'beloved' by manufacturers of television remote controls.

Deans

Scottish surname. The name sometimes originates from the English surname Dean (which derives from the English word *dene* meaning 'valley'), but was also taken up by servants of people who held the ecclesiastical position of dean. Famous people called Deans include Scottish rugby captain Colin Deans.

Denholm

Scottish surname and occasional male first name.
The name originates from the Borders village of
Denholm, near Hawick, which in turn comes from
the Old English words *den* meaning 'valley' and
holm meaning either 'dry land' or 'island'. Famous
Denholms include actor Denholm Elliott, who
starred in two of the *Indiana Jones* films and was
awarded a CBE for his services to acting.

Dewar

Scottish surname that derives from the Gaelic
deoradh and means 'pilgrim'. Famous Dewars include
James Dewar, who invented the thermos or vacuum
flask, Donald Dewar, the first First Minister of the
reconvened Scottish Parliament, and Dewar's blended
whisky.

Dickson

Popular surname in Scotland. The name derives from
Dick, the diminutive form of Richard. The name
Richard was brought to Britain by the Normans, but
has Germanic origins (with *ric* meaning 'power' and
hard meaning 'hardy' or 'strong'). Famous Scottish
Dicksons include one of the *Two Fat Ladies*, Clarissa
Dickson Wright, and the somewhat slimmer Barbara

Dickson, who is Scotland's most successful female recording artist ever.

Docherty

Scottish surname that derives from the Gaelic *dochart* meaning 'one who suffers'. Docherty is also a variation of the Irish surname Doherty, which has the similar meaning of 'not loved'. Famous Scottish Dochertys include football manager Tommy Docherty who was 'not loved' by several football clubs, as he was sacked numerous times in his career.

Donald

Male first name that comes from the Gaelic and means 'world-ruler'. Diminutives of Donald include Don, Donny, and Donnie and famous Donalds include Australian cricketer Donald Bradman, world speed record holder Donald Campbell, film star Donald Sutherland, American politician and businessman Donald Rumsfeld, American billionaire Donald Trump (whose mother comes from Lewis), American singer Donny Osmond, and Scotland's first First Minister Donald Dewar. The name is also familiar from cult film *Donnie Darko* and long-standing Disney cartoon character Donald Duck (who has a Scottish uncle called Scrooge McDuck, and so is presumably of Scottish descent).

Donald is also the name of the kilt-wearing hero of the song 'Donald, Where's Your Trousers?', who despite being both not very big and awfully shy proves very popular with the ladies.

Dougal

Male first name that is an anglicized form of the Gaelic name *Dubhghall* meaning 'dark stranger' and thought to be given to individuals of foreign origin. Famous Dougals include Scottish mountaineer Dougal Haston, Father Dougal McGuire from the sitcom *Father Ted*, and the central character of the classic children's television programme *The Magic Roundabout*.

Douglas

Surname and male first name, as well as a Borders clan. The name Douglas derives from a place in Lanarkshire that means 'dark water', coming from the Gaelic *dubh* meaning 'dark' or 'black' and *glais* meaning 'water' or 'stream'. Diminutives of the first name Douglas include Doug and Dougie.

The Douglas family were supporters of Robert the Bruce and were rewarded with land. The 'Black' Douglases became the most powerful family in Scotland in the 14th century, and remained one of the most prominent families in Lanarkshire, the Borders, and Angus.

Famous people called Douglas include British Prime Minister Alec Douglas-Home, American general Douglas MacArthur, wartime pilot Douglas Bader, author of *The Hitchhikers Guide to the Galaxy* Douglas Adams, and two father-and-son Hollywood dynasties: Douglas Fairbanks and Douglas Fairbanks Junior, and Kirk and Michael Douglas. Despite his very Scottish name, Kirk Douglas was actually born Issur Danielovitch and is of Russian–Jewish origin.

Castle Douglas is a town in Dumfries and Galloway that was developed by merchant William Douglas in the 18th century. In fact, there is no castle in the town, although the ruined 14th-century Douglas stronghold of Threave Castle is only two miles away.

Drummond

Scottish surname that originates from the village of Drymen near Loch Lomond. The name Drymen derives from the Gaelic *drumain* meaning 'on the ridge'. Famous Drummonds include Captain Hugh Drummond (better known as Bulldog Drummond) who appeared in a series of adventure novels and films in the 1920s and 1930s.

Duncan

Male first name and surname that derives from the Gaelic name *Donnchadh* or *Donnachie* meaning 'brown-haired warrior'. Famous Duncans include flamboyant American dancer Isadora Duncan, English footballer Duncan Edwards, who died in the 1958 Munich air crash aged only 21, and short-lived Conservative Party leader Iain Duncan Smith. Two of Scotland's earliest kings were called Duncan, and it was Duncan I who was the King Duncan killed by Macbeth in Shakespeare's play.

Dunlop

Scottish surname that originates from the place in Ayrshire called Dunlop. The place name derives from the Gaelic *dun* meaning 'fort' and either *luib* meaning 'bend' (referring to the bend of a river), or else *lapach* meaning 'muddy'. Famous Dunlops include Scottish inventor John Boyd Dunlop, who invented the pneumatic tyre and gave his name to the multinational Dunlop tyre company.

Eilidh

Female first name that is the Gaelic form of Ellen or Helen, which means 'bright one' or 'light' in Greek.

Eilidh is currently one of the most popular girls' names in Scotland.

Elizabeth

Female first name that has been popular in Scotland for centuries. The name derives from the Greek *Elisabet*, which in turn comes from the Hebrew *Elisheva* meaning 'God is my oath'. There are numerous diminutives of Elizabeth including Bess, Bet, Betty, Beth, Elspeth, Elsie, Libby, Liz, Lizzie, and Liza. In the 20th century Elizabeth has become associated with British royalty through the current queen Elizabeth II and her mother Elizabeth, the Queen Mother, whose father was the Earl of Strathmore and who was brought up in Glamis Castle in Angus.

Elliot

Surname and male first name that is found throughout Britain, but in Scotland is associated with the Borders and the formidable Clan Elliot. The name Elliot is of uncertain origin, but it has been suggested that it comes from a place called Eliot in Forfar, or that is a Scottish variation of the English surname *Elwold*, or else a Norman variation of the Hebrew name *Elias*. The spelling 'Elliot' is considered to be the Scottish version in comparison with the

English spelling 'Elliott'. Famous Elliots include Mamas and Papas singer Mama Cass Elliot and the eponymous hero of *Billy Elliot*, the film about the ballet-dancing son of a Scottish miner.

Elspeth

Scottish variation of Elizabeth. The name became a female first name in its own right but has largely fallen out of fashion. Diminutives include Elspie and Elsie, and Elsie Inglis was a pioneering surgeon and suffragette who set up a maternity hospital for the poor in Edinburgh.

Ewan, Ewen, Euan

Male first name that comes from a Gaelic name *Eoghan* that is of obscure origin, but might possibly mean 'of the yew tree' or 'youth'. Ewan and Euan are also variants of John and Iain. Famous Ewans include Ewan McGregor, Scottish star of *Trainspotting* and the later *Star Wars* films, and folk singer Ewan MacColl.

Ewing

Surname that derives from the male first name Ewan. The name Ewing is associated with two famous dynasties: the Scottish Ewings, led by Winnie Ewing, who have given us four members of either the

Westminster or Holyrood parliaments, and the *Dallas* Ewings, led by Jock and Miss Ellie Ewing, who have given us numerous prominent Texan oilmen.

Farquhar, Farquharson

Male first name and related surname. The name Farquhar is derived from the Gaelic *fear* meaning 'man' and the Gaelic *car* meaning 'well-loved'. The surname Farquharson means simply 'son of Farquhar'. The Farquharsons were a prominent Aberdeenshire clan.

Fergus

Male first name and surname that comes from the Gaelic and means 'man of strength' or 'chosen man'. Fergus was a common name in the royal families of both the Picts and the original Scots who came to Scotland from Ireland and founded the kingdom of Dalriada. Fergus MacErc (or Fergus of Ulster) is traditionally believed to have been the first king of Dalriada in the 5th century.

Ferguson

Surname that means 'son of Fergus'. Famous Fergusons include football manager Alex Ferguson, ex-royal Sarah Ferguson, and Stacy Ann Ferguson of the Black Eyed Peas – all of whom are nicknamed 'Fergie'. Scottish comedian turned American chat show host Craig Ferguson is not, however, known by this nickname, although he did once go by the pseudonym of Bing Hitler.

Finlay, Findlay

Surname and male first name. Finlay derives from the Gaelic name *Fionnlach* meaning 'fair warrior'. Famous Finlays include Doctor John Finlay from *Doctor Finlay's Casebook*, British Lions rugby captain Finlay Calder, and actor Frank Finlay.

Finn, Fingal

Male first name. Finn is a diminutive of both *Fingal* meaning 'fair stranger' and *Finlay* meaning 'fair warrior', and can also be a name in its own right, coming from the Gaelic name *Fionn* meaning 'fair'. The popularity of the name derives from Fionn mac Cumhaill (or Finn McCool), who was a legendary Celtic warrior prominent first in Irish mythology and then later in Scottish mythology through the hugely popular *Ossian* poems by 18th-century Scottish writer James Macpherson (where he was given the name Fingal).

The name Fingal was later given to a huge sea

cave on the uninhabited island of Staffa and was made internationally famous by composer Felix Mendelssohn, who visited Fingal's Cave in 1829 and would later compose the *Hebrides Overture* (better known throughout the world as *Fingal's Cave*).

Fiona

Scottish girls' first name. Fiona is the feminine form of the Gaelic *Fionn* meaning 'fair' or 'white'. The popularity of the name is thought to be due to its use by James Macpherson in his 18th-century *Ossian* poems and by 19th-century writer William Sharp, who used Fiona MacLeod as his pen name, for there was no previous tradition of Fiona being used as a girls' name. Fiona became a very common first name in Scotland in the 20th century, even though not all Fionas are blonde.

Famous Fionas include newsreader and *Antiques Roadshow* presenter Fiona Bruce, who despite her name is not Scottish.

An even more famous Fiona is Princess Fiona from the *Shrek* films. Despite having a Scottish name, Princess Fiona is not Scottish, although her husband Shrek does have a Scottish accent (sort of).

Fleming

Surname that originated in Scotland in Lanarkshire. The name derives from Flemish immigrants from Flanders, in what is now Belgium. Famous Flemings include Scottish inventor of penicillin Alexander Fleming, American film director of *Gone with the Wind* and *The Wizard of Oz* Victor Fleming, and *James Bond* and *Chitty Chitty Bang Bang* creator Ian Fleming.

Flora

Female first name. The name is associated with Scotland through Jacobite heroine Flora MacDonald, who in 1746 helped Bonnie Prince Charlie escape to Skye by disguising him as her maid. The name Flora is that of the Roman goddess of flowers and spring, whose name is related to *flos*, the Latin name for a flower. In Scotland, however, Flora was the anglicized form of the Gaelic *Fionnaghal*, and is the feminine form of Fingal and Finn. The popular brand of British margarine called Flora may be 'fair', but has no connection with Scotland.

Forbes

Surname and occasional male first name. The Forbes family originated in Aberdeenshire and the name derives from the Gaelic *forba* meaning 'field'. The American *Forbes* magazine was founded in New York in 1917 by B.C. Forbes, who was born in Aberdeenshire, and publishes the annual *Forbes 400* list of the wealthiest people in America.

Forsyth

Popular surname from Lowland Scotland. The name has unknown origins: it has been suggested that it may possibly derive from a French place name, but it is generally thought that it either derives from the Gaelic word *fothar* meaning 'woodland' or another Gaelic word *fearsidhe* meaning 'man of peace' (referring to a priest). Famous Forsyths include television star Bruce Forsyth, American actor John Forsythe (who played Blake Carrington in *Dynasty* and was the voice of Charlie in *Charlie's Angels*), thriller writer Frederick Forsyth, and Scottish film director Bill Forsyth (famous for *Gregory's Girl* and *Local Hero*).

Fraser

Scottish surname (also found in the form Frazer) and male first name. The name is of uncertain origin but either comes from a Norman name de Friselle (or de Fresel), from the Dutch region of Frisia (meaning 'a Frisian'), or from the French world *fraise* (meaning

'strawberry'). The Frasers became established in the Peebles area in the 11th century before moving to the north-east. One of Scotland's best-known castles, Castle Fraser, was built by the family in Aberdeenshire in the 16th century.

Famous Frasers include star of *The Mummy* films Brendan Fraser, former Australian Prime Minister Malcolm Fraser, author of the *Flashman* novels George MacDonald Fraser, and the doom-laden Private Frazer from *Dad's Army*.

Fraser River is the longest river in British Columbia in Canada, and Fraser Island off the Queensland coast of Australia is the largest sand island in the world. The fishing town of Fraserburgh on the north-east coast of Scotland was named after the local landowner Alexander Fraser.

Galloway

Scottish surname that derives from the region and former kingdom of Galloway in south-west Scotland. The place name comes from the Gaelic *Gall-Gadal* and means 'land of the Gaelic-Norse' in recognition of the Scandinavian influence in the region from the 9th to the 11th century.

Famous Galloways include Scottish politician and radio host George Galloway, who is affectionately known as 'Gorgeous' – although not necessarily by his many political opponents.

Garry

Male first name that is a variation of the English name Gary. The English name is of Germanic origin, meaning 'spear', and became popular in the 20th century when a young American actor called Frank Cooper changed his name to Gary Cooper and became a huge Hollywood star, with *High Noon* being his most famous film. The form Garry is also associated with Scotland through the Perthshire and Highland place names of the River Garry, Loch Garry, and Glen Garry. In these names, Garry is of ancient Celtic or Pictish origin and is thought to mean 'rough'.

Gavin

Male first name. The name was found elsewhere in Britain and Ireland, but retained its popularity only in Scotland and is now considered a predominantly Scottish name. The name derives from the name *Gawain*, name of the nephew of King Arthur who was one of the most illustrious of the Knights of the Round Table. It is thought that the name *Gawain* may be Welsh in origin and means 'white hawk'. Famous Scottish Gavins include author of *Ring of*

Bright Water Gavin Maxwell and Scottish rugby captain Gavin Hastings. In recent years, the most famous Gavin in Britain has been Gavin Shipman, who is married to Stacey West in the comedy *Gavin and Stacey* – although to his best mate Smithy he is known as 'Gav-lah'.

George

Male first name that has been popular in Scotland since the 18th century and is associated with royalty through the six British kings of that name. The first King George became monarch in 1714, displacing the Stewarts as the royal family of Britain. George I came from Hanover in Germany but the name originates from the Greek name *Georgios* meaning 'farmer'. Geordie and Dod are diminutives of George.

The name features prominently in Scotland's major cities, with George Streets in Edinburgh and Aberdeen, and George Square at the heart of Glasgow's city centre.

Georgina

Female first name that originated in Scotland in the 18th century. The name was used by supporters of the Hanoverian monarchy as the feminine form of George.

Gilchrist

Scottish surname that derives from the Gaelic word
gille meaning 'servant'. The name thus means 'servant
of Christ'. Famous Gilchrists include Australian
cricketer Adam Gilchrist.

Giles

Male first name that derives from the Greek *Aigidios*
meaning 'young goat'. Although the name has never
been as popular in Scotland as it has in England,
Saint Giles is the patron saint of Edinburgh and
the mostly 14th-century St Giles' Cathedral played
a prominent part in the Scottish Reformation,
with John Knox being its first Protestant minister
(although its official name is the High Kirk
of Edinburgh). Saint Giles was a 7th-century
Greek-born saint who settled in France and is the
patron saint of cripples and lepers.

When Edinburgh's New Town was being planned in
the late 18th century, St Giles Street was the original
choice for what would become Edinburgh's principal
street. However royal politics intervened and the
planned St Giles Street was eventually called Princes
Street.

Gillespie

Scottish surname that derives from the Gaelic *gille easbuig* meaning 'servant of the bishop'. This harks back to the pre-Reformation days when the Scottish church had bishops. Famous Gillespies include Scottish singer Bobby Gillespie, a member of the group Primal Scream, and American John Birks Gillespie, who is better known as jazz trumpeter Dizzy Gillespie.

Glen, Glenn

Surname and male (or occasionally female) first name that derives from the Gaelic *glean* meaning 'valley'. Famous Glenns include American band-leader Glenn Miller, American astronaut-turned-politician John Glenn, American country singer Glen Campbell, Australian cricketer Glenn McGrath, and American actress Glenn Close.

Gordon

Surname and male first name. The Gordon family has been associated with the north-east of Scotland since the 13th century, but the name originates from a place name in the Borders that means either 'hill fort' or 'great fort'.

Gordon has given its name to the Scottish regiment

the Gordon Highlanders, the Scottish dance called the Gay Gordons (which was also the nickname of the Gordon Highlanders), and Gordon's gin, which was first produced by one Alexander Gordon in 1769, and which has been happily imbibed over the centuries by Gordon Highlanders and non-Gordon Highlanders alike.

Famous Gordons include General Charles Gordon, who died failing to defend Khartoum in the Sudan in 1885, singer Gordon Sumner (better known as Sting from The Police), Prime Minister and former Chancellor of the Exchequer Gordon Brown, television chef Gordon Ramsay, Police Commissioner Gordon from the cartoon *Batman* (first name Jim), and another comic-strip character, Flash Gordon. The poet Lord Byron was born George Gordon Byron and spent part of his childhood in Aberdeen, which might explain why he later became known as 'mad, bad, and dangerous to know'. Robert Gordon was a benefactor of the city of Aberdeen and the city's Robert Gordon University is named after him.

The popularity of Gordon as a first name noticeably declined after 1978 when the singer Jilted John had a hit single, also called 'Jilted John', which featured the chorus of 'Gordon is a moron'.

Graham, Grahame, Graeme

Scottish surname and male first name. The name derives from the Anglo-Norman noble family de Graham who came to Scotland in the 12th century bringing a surname that may have originated from the Lincolnshire town of Grantham (later to be the home town of a certain Margaret Thatcher), which means 'gravel settlement'.

The Grahams became established in Lothian, Strathearn, and Montrose, and have played a major part in Scottish history as supporters of the Stewarts, with James Graham, the Marquis of Montrose, leading the Scottish Royalist forces in the Civil Wars of the 1640s, and John Graham, known as 'Bonnie Dundee', leading the first Jacobite uprising in Scotland in support of the deposed James VII in 1689 – both Montrose and Dundee would eventually be defeated.

Other famous Scottish Grahams include inventor of the telephone Alexander Graham Bell, author of *The Wind in the Willows* Kenneth Grahame, and footballer Graeme Souness. Famous non-Scottish Grahams include American evangelist Billy Graham, novelist Graham Greene, cricketer Graham Gooch, comedian and presenter Graham Norton, and the very Scottish-sounding film star Heather Graham (who actually comes from Milwaukee).

Grant

Male first name and surname. The name Grant derives from the French word *grand* meaning 'large' and the Grant clan was concentrated in Banff. Famous Grants include film stars Cary Grant and Hugh Grant, reggae star Eddy Grant, American Civil War General and President Ulysses S. Grant, and Grant Mitchell from *EastEnders*. Grant's is a well known producer of blended whisky.

The Highland town of Grantown-on-Spey is named after the Grant family.

Gray

Surname that is the Scottish spelling of the English Grey. The name comes from the colour and as a surname means 'grey-haired'. Famous Grays include American actress Linda Gray, who played Sue Ellen in *Dallas*, Scottish broadcaster Muriel Gray, Greyfriars' Bobby's master John Gray, and the title character of Oscar Wilde's novel *The Picture of Dorian Gray*. The medical reference book *Gray's Anatomy* was named after an English anatomist Henry Gray, who had the Scottish spelling, and is different from the American television series *Grey's Anatomy*, which doesn't.

Greer

Surname and female first name derived from the Scottish surnames Grier and Grierson, which were themselves originally contractions of Gregor or MacGregor. Famous Greers include Australian writer Germaine Greer and Hollywood actress Greer Garson, who took her first name from her mother's maiden name.

Gregor

Male first name and surname that is the Scottish version of Gregory. The name means 'watchful' in its original Greek and also occurs in the famous clan surname MacGregor. A common diminutive of Gregor is Greg. Famous Gregors include actor Gregor Fisher, who is best known for playing the character of Rab C. Nesbitt.

Greig

Scottish surname that derives from the surname MacGregor and from the first name and surname Gregor. Famous Greigs include footballer John Greig, *Black Books* and *Archers* actress Tamsin Greig, and cricketer Tony Greig. Norwegian composer of *Peer Gynt* Edvard Grieg was descended from Scottish Greigs who had emigrated to Norway.

The surname Gregg is an English variation of Gregory and, despite what many people think, the firm of Greggs the bakers is not Scottish but comes from Newcastle.

Grieve

Surname that originated in the Borders. The name does not (as one might expect) derive from mourning or grave-digging, but from the English word *greve* meaning 'steward' or 'estate manager'. Famous Grieves include poet Christopher Grieve, who is better known as one of Scotland's greatest poets, Hugh MacDiarmid.

Gunn

Scottish surname that originated in Caithness. The name comes from the Norse word *gunnar* meaning 'warrior' (as found in the name of Norwegian footballer Ole Gunnar Solskjaer). Famous Gunns include *Treasure Island* character Ben Gunn, Scottish novelist Neil Gunn, and the Duane Eddy instrumental hit single 'Peter Gunn'.

Guthrie

Scottish surname that originates from a village in Angus. The place name is derived from the Gaelic *gaoth* or *gaothair* and means 'windy place'. Famous Guthries include American folk singer Woody Guthrie, who wrote the song 'This Land Is Your Land' and was idolized by the young Bob Dylan, and Chris Guthrie, the main character of Lewis Grassic Gibbon's *A Scots Quair* trilogy.

Haig

Scottish surname that became established in the Borders but originated as a Norman name. The origins of the name are in several places whose names included the Norse word *hagi* meaning 'enclosure'. Famous Haigs included Douglas Haig, the controversial Scottish commander of the British army in the First World War (after whom the Earl Haig Poppy Fund is named), and Alexander Haig, the American soldier who served as Secretary of State in the 1980s.

Hamilton

Scottish surname and occasional male first name. Hamilton derives from the Norman family of de Hameldon. They took their name from the Hampshire town of Hambledon, whose name derives from the Old English *hamel dun* meaning 'crooked hill'.

The Clan Hamilton would become established in Lanarkshire. They were given the title of Duke of Hamilton in 1643, and the Lanarkshire town of Cadzow was renamed Hamilton in honour of the Duke. Two other large towns named Hamilton can be found in Ontario, Canada, and North Island, New Zealand, and Hamilton is also the name of the capital of Bermuda.

Famous Hamiltons include American founding father Alexander Hamilton, Horatio Nelson's mistress Lady Emma Hamilton (who was actually married to a Scottish diplomat called William Hamilton at the time), *Terminator* star Linda Hamilton, and motor-racing driver Lewis Hamilton.

Hamish

Male first name. Hamish is the anglicized version of *Seumas*, which is in turn the Gaelic for James. Hamish is often considered an archetypal Highland name and famous Hamishes include the title character of the television series *Hamish MacBeth*, which starred Robert Carlyle as a Highland policeman, and the hero of the popular comic strip *Hot Shot Hamish*, a Hebridean footballer with the most powerful right foot in the world.

Hannay

Scottish surname that originated in Galloway.
The name possibly derives from the Irish surname
O'Hannaidh that means 'son of Annach' (with
Annach being an Irish first name of uncertain
meaning) and in Ireland has been anglicized to
Hanna. Famous Hannays include Richard Hannay,
the Scottish-born hero of *The Thirty-Nine Steps* and
several other John Buchan novels.

Harkness

Scottish surname that became established in
Dumfries and Galloway. The name is of uncertain
origin, but probably derives from an Old English first
name *Hereca* combined with the Old English *naess* or
Norse *nes* meaning 'headland'. Famous people called
Harkness include Captain Jack Harkness from the
television series *Torchwood*.

Harris

Surname and male first name. Harris is the southern
part of the island of Lewis and Harris in the Outer
Hebrides (and not, as many people think, a separate
island, even though it is usually referred to as the
Isle of Harris). The Gaelic name for Harris is *Na
Hearadh*, but the name originally comes from the

Old Norse *Haerri* meaning 'higher island', as Harris has more high hills than Lewis to the north.

Harris and Harrison have long been common English and Welsh surnames, derived from the first name Henry, but they have no connection with the Scottish Harris. However, the famous cloth called Harris Tweed is named after the Isle of Harris and has been hand-woven there since the 19th century.

Lewis has become a very popular boys' name in Scotland in recent years, and Harris has slowly been following in its footsteps, with the pair of names being ideal for twin boys.

Hay

Surname that means 'hedge', whether from the Old English word *haeg* or the French word *haia*. In the case of the French word, it was the Norman family of de la Haye who brought the name to Britain. The Hays in Scotland became established in Perthshire.

Heather

Scottish female first name, coming from the shrub with pink and white flowers that is found throughout Scotland. Famous Heathers include former Mrs McCartney, Heather Mills, American television star Heather Locklear, American film star Heather

Graham, and Scottish meteorologist Heather
'The Weather' Reid (who has yet to find fame in
Hollywood or marry a Beatle).

Henderson

Surname found throughout Britain, but long popular
in Scotland. The name derives from 'son of Henry'
or 'son of Hendry' with Hendry being the Scottish
variant of Henry. The name Henry itself comes
from the French name *Henri* and originally was the
Germanic *Heinrich* meaning 'ruler of an enclosure'.

Hendrie, Hendry

Scottish form of the male first name Henry. The
name Henry came to Britain from the French *Henri*
and originates from the German *Heinrich* meaning
'ruler of an enclosure'. Famous Hendrys include seven
times world snooker champion Stephen Hendry.

Heriot, Herriot

Scottish surname that originates from the Midlothian
village of Heriot. The village takes its name from
the medieval English word *heriot*, which has the
complicated legal meaning of 'land or some other
form of death duty paid or given to the lord on the
death of a tenant'.

Famous Heriots include Scottish financier and philanthropist George Heriot, who was given the name 'Jinglin' Geordie' in reference to his wealth and after whom (alongside inventor James Watt) Edinburgh's Heriot-Watt University was named in 1966. Famous Herriots include vet and best-selling author James Herriot (brought up and educated in Glasgow under his real name James Alfred Wight), whose books inspired the popular television series *All Creatures Great and Small*.

Hislop

Surname from Lowland Scotland. The name comes from the Norse word *hasl* meaning 'hazel' and the Old English word *hope* meaning 'hollow' or 'grove'. Famous Hislops include *Have I Got News for You* captain Ian Hislop.

Home, Hume

Scottish surname. The name is either a variation of the English surname Holm (which derives from the Old English *holm* and Norse *holmr* and means either 'island dweller' or 'dweller on dry land', but can also mean 'water meadow') or else derives from the place called Home in Berwickshire (which may have the same derivation).

The Homes became established in the Borders and the Earls of Home are a prominent Border family. The 14th Earl of Home was Alec Douglas-Home, who was a short-lived British Prime Minister from 1963 to 1964. Other famous Humes include renowned Scottish philosopher David Hume, Northern Irish politician John Hume, and Scottish model Kirsty Hume.

Both Home and Hume are pronounced 'hume' in Scotland.

Houston

Scottish surname that takes its name from the village of Houston in Renfrewshire. The village was named after a 12th-century Norman landowner Hugh de Padinam (the name is literally 'Hugh's town'). Famous people called Houston include American singers Whitney Houston and Thelma Houston, who sang 'Don't Leave Me This Way'.

American general and politician Sam Houston led the Texan army in its War of Independence with Mexico and became the first President of the short-lived independent state of Texas. The city of Houston is named after him and is the largest city in the state and the fourth-largest in the United States.

The phrase 'Houston, we have a problem' does not

refer to the recent career of Whitney, but rather to Mission Control at the NASA Space Centre in the city of Houston, and in particular the aborted 1970 Apollo XIII mission to the moon. The phrase is in fact a misquotation, as what astronauts Jim Lovell and John Swigert actually said after a major explosion took place on the spacecraft was, 'Houston, we've had a problem.'

Hugh

Male first name that was brought to England by the Normans. The name is Germanic in origin, deriving from the word *hug* meaning 'heart' or 'mind'. In Scotland, Hugh is also the anglicized form of the Gaelic name *Aodh* meaning 'fire', which as a surname has been anglicized to MacKay. Scottish diminutives of Hugh include Hughie, Shughie, and Shug.

Famous Scottish Hughs include poet Hugh MacDiarmid, while English actors Hugh Grant and Hugh Laurie both come from Scottish families.

Hunter

Surname that is found throughout Britain and takes its name from the occupation of huntsman or hunter. In Scotland, Hunters became established in Ayrshire and famous Scottish Hunters include surgeon

William Hunter, after whom the Hunterian Museum
and Art Gallery in Glasgow is named.

Hutton

Predominantly Scottish surname that is derived
from the Old English *hoh* meaning 'ridge' and *ton*
meaning 'settlement'. Famous Huttons include
Scottish 'Father of Geology' James Hutton and Irish
judge Brian Hutton, who became best known for the
controversial Hutton Report of 2004 investigating
the events surrounding the death of weapons expert
David Kelly. Famous English cricket captain Len
Hutton came from the Yorkshire branch of the
family.

Ian, Iain

Male first names that are Scottish forms for John
meaning 'God is gracious'. Iain is the Gaelic form
of the name, and Ian is an anglicization of Iain. For
most of the 20th century, Ian was the most popular
boys' name of Gaelic origin in Scotland. Famous Ians
include James Bond creator Ian Fleming, cricketer
and Shredded Wheat fan Ian Botham, author Ian
McEwan, Northern Ireland politician Ian Paisley, Joy
Division singer Ian Curtis, footballer Ian Rush, editor
of *Private Eye* Ian Hislop, and Gandalf himself, actor
Ian McKellen.

Inglis

Scottish surname that originated in the Lowlands. The name is derived from the Scots for 'an English person' or 'an English-speaking person'. Famous people called Inglis include Scottish suffragette and pioneering surgeon Elsie Inglis.

Inkster

Surname that originated in Shetland. The name comes from a Norse place name *Ingsetter* meaning 'Ing's settlement'. Famous Inskters include American golfer Juli Inkster.

Innes

Scottish male first name and surname that means 'island-dweller'. The name comes from the Gaelic word *inis* meaning 'islet'. The name originated in Moray at a place named Innes, and famous people called Innes include comedy writer Neil Innes from the Bonzo Dog Doo Dah Band.

Interestingly, the Scottish surname MacInnes does not mean 'son of an islander', but means 'son of Kenneth', with Innes here being the anglicized form of *Aonghus*, which is the Gaelic form of Kenneth.

Iona

Female first name. The name comes from the small island of Iona in the Inner Hebrides, a spiritual centre and place of pilgrimage and learning since Saint Columba travelled from Ireland and set up his first monastery there in 563. Many of the earliest Scottish kings were buried in Iona and Labour leader John Smith was buried there in 1994. Iona Abbey was extensively restored in the 19th and the 20th centuries, and Iona remains a popular destination for both Christian and non-Christian visitors.

The name of the island either derives from the Norse word *ey* (that simply means 'island') or an Irish word *eo* (which is thought to mean 'yew tree'). Over the years the two have been combined to give 'island of yew trees', as the yew was associated with holy places.

Irvine, Irving

Surname and occasional male first name. Irvine takes its name from the town in Ayrshire, which in turn takes its name from the River Irvine. The name either means 'white river' or 'brown river', and famous Irvines include American authors Washington Irving (who wrote the stories 'Rip Van Winkle' and 'The Legend of Sleepy Hollow') and John Irving (who wrote *The World According to Garp*), Scottish rugby player Andy Irvine, and *Trainspotting* author

Irvine Welsh. Irving Berlin is the name of one of
the most famous songwriters in the world, with
his best-known song being 'White Christmas', but
he adopted the name Irving to replace his original
Belarussian name of Israel Baline.

Isla

Scottish girls' name. The current popularity of Isla
in Scotland probably comes from modern fashion
for using Scottish islands as first names. The name
is derived from the Island of Islay in the Inner
Hebrides, which is famed for its whisky. Originally,
however, the name is believed to have referred to
the Glen and River Isla in Perthshire. The meaning
of both Isla and Islay is unclear, however, with Isla
thought to be Brythonic in origin and Islay thought
to be Norse, perhaps named after somebody called
Ile. Famous Islas include *Generation Game* co-host
Isla St Clair and Australian actress Isla Fisher.

Jack

Popular male first name and surname, but with
different origins. As a male first name, Jack is a
diminutive of John, which means 'God is gracious'
and John was for centuries the most popular male
first name in Scotland as well as the rest of the
English-speaking world. In recent years Jack has

become a popular male first name in its own right and now vies with Lewis as the most popular name for boys in Scotland.

Jack is also a predominantly Scottish surname. In this context it does not derive from John, but from the first name *Jakke*, a diminutive of *Jacques*, which is the French form of both James and Jacob and means 'supplanter'.

Jackson

Surname that means 'son of Jack'. Famous Scottish Jacksons include actor Gordon Jackson, who starred in *Upstairs, Downstairs* and *The Professionals*.

James

Biblical male name that derives from another Biblical name, Jacob, and is thought to mean 'supplanter'. James has long been a popular name in Scotland through its royal traditions. In the period between 1400 and 1625, six out of the seven Scottish monarchs were called James. (The seventh was not called James because she was a girl.) James VI of Scotland became James I of England in 1603, so uniting the two Crowns under one monarch. After James VII of Scotland (James II of England) was deposed in 1688, supporters of James and his son (also James) and grandson (known as the Old and Young Pretender respectively) were called Jacobites (after *Jacobus*, the Latin form of James).

Other famous Scots called James include steam-engine innovator James Watt, world renowned physicist James Clerk Maxwell, and author of *Peter Pan* James Barrie. Diminutives of James include Jim, Jamesie, Jimmie, and Jimmy (a form which deserves a separate entry to itself).

Jameson, Jamieson

Predominantly Scottish surname that means 'son of James'. Famous Jamesons include Jameson's Irish Whiskey, which was first distilled in Dublin in 1780 by a Scotsman called John Jameson.

Jamie

Male and female first name that is the Scottish diminutive for James, but has become a very popular name in its own right. Famous Jamies include female film star Jamie Lee Curtis, male film star Jamie Foxx, and television chef Jamie Oliver.

Jardine

Scottish surname that originated in Dumfries. The name is derived from the French word *jardin*

meaning 'garden'. Famous Jardines include Scottish
doctor William Jardine, who founded the Jardine
Matheson company that helped establish Hong Kong
as a major world trading centre, Al Jardine from
the Beach Boys, and DCI Michael Jardine from the
television series *Taggart*.

Jean

Female first name that was introduced to Britain
from the French *Jehane* and is a feminine form of
John. While the name fell out of favour in England
(where it was replaced by Jane), Jean remained a
popular first name in Scotland and became regarded
as a typically Scottish name. Famous Scottish Jeans
include the much put-upon wife of Robert Burns,
Jean Armour, and the heroine of the classic book
and film *The Prime of Miss Jean Brodie*. Other
famous Jeans include the actress Jean Alexander,
who played Hilda Ogden in *Coronation Street* for
many years, original 1930s Hollywood blonde
bombshell Jean Harlow, Norma Jean Baker (the
real name of Harlow's successor Marilyn Monroe),
and former Wimbledon champion Billie-Jean King.
'Billie Jean' was also the name of one of Michael
Jackson's biggest hit singles, but the song has (as far
as we know) no connection with the bespectacled
tennis player.

Diminutives of Jean include Jeannie and Jessie. 'Jeanie with the Light Brown Hair' was a well-known song by Stephen Foster that began with the words 'I dream of Jeannie', a line that would reappear in the 1960s as the name of a popular American television comedy.

Jessie

Scottish female first name that was mostly used as a diminutive of Jean or Janet (both of which are feminine forms of John), but can also be a first name in its own right. Famous Scottish Jessies include author Jessie Kesson.

It is not clear whether Jessies were generally taller or bigger-boned than your average Scottish Mary or Margaret, but when men searched for a female name to insult a fellow who was considered weak or insufficiently masculine, it was the name Jessie that they chose to use. Over time, the term 'Jessie' turned into 'you big Jessie' and, whether coincidentally or not, Jessie soon went out of fashion as a Scottish girls' name.

Jimmy

Popular diminutive of the name James (which is discussed in its own entry). The name James and its diminutive were so pervasive in Scotland that 'Jimmy' was used by Scottish men as a friendly term of address for any man whose name was unknown, as there would be a high probability that Jimmy would actually be the stranger's name.

This use of the word 'Jimmy' fell out of favour in Scotland in the 1980s when English comedian Russ Abbot invented a character called C.U. Jimmy, an unintelligible, red-headed, kilted caricature of a Scotsman, not especially complimentary either to Scots or people named James. However in a post-ironic twist, the 'See You Jimmy hat', a tartan bonnet with attached orange fright wig, was later adopted by Scotland's Tartan Army at home and abroad as a proud symbol of the Scottish nation. The hat will often play 'Scotland the Brave' when you press the bobble on top.

Jock

Popular diminutive of the name John (which is discussed in its own entry). The name Jock is commonly used by non-Scots to describe all Scots — no matter what their actual name or gender may be — often in a not especially flattering manner.

In modern American English, the term 'jock' refers (not always as a compliment) to a young male known for his aptitude for sport (especially sports such as

American football, baseball, and basketball), often with a suggestion that this is in inverse proportion to his academic ability. The name comes from the jockstraps (originally named 'jockey straps') that sportsmen wear to protect the more sensitive parts of their anatomy. Not surprisingly, the name Jock has become much less popular in recent years.

Famous Jocks include Celtic and Scotland football manager Jock Stein, original *Dallas* patriarch Jock Ewing, and Jock Tamson of whom the phrase 'We're a' Jock Tamson's bairns' is coined, expressing a common humanity to one and all.

Another famous Jock, and perhaps showing an example of how the name became so prevalent, was the somewhat frisky Jock who featured in the popular Harry Lauder song 'Stop Yer Tickling, Jock'.

John

Male first name derived from the Hebrew meaning 'God is gracious'. For centuries John was the most popular male first name in Scotland. In the Bible it was the name of both John the Baptist and Saint John, one of the twelve disciples. Diminutives of John include Jack and Jock (both discussed in their own entries) as well as Jocky.

Famous Scottish Johns include the unfortunate John

Balliol, who was deposed as Scottish king by the English in 1296 only four years after they had chosen him in the first place, inventor of the television John Logie Baird, Labour leader John Smith, founder of the BBC John Reith, conservationist John Muir, and author of *The Thirty-Nine Steps* John Buchan.

Another very famous Scottish John is John o' Groats, known as being the most northerly village in the Scottish and British mainland, and the starting point of all cross-British journeys, although John o' Groats was in fact not a Scot but a 15th-century Dutchman Jan de Groot, who ran the ferry to Orkney.

Johnston, Johnstone

Scottish surnames that sound identical but had different origins. Johnston is a Scots variation of English surname Johnson, meaning 'son of John'. Johnstone derives from the Scots word *toun* and means 'the town of John'. Saint Johnstone is an old name for Perth that still survives in the town's football team, and Johnstone is a town in Renfrewshire. Over the years, however, the two names became intermingled.

In medieval Scotland, the Johnstone clan was one of the important clans in the Borders, boasting the somewhat unlikely nickname of 'the Gentle Johnstones'. Famous Johnstons and Johnstones

include cricket commentator Brian Johnston and Celtic footballer Jimmy Johnstone.

Kayleigh

Female first name. The name became popular in 1985 when British rock band Marillion reached number two in the charts with a song of that name. Almost all Kayleighs in the United Kingdom were born after 1985, and name became particularly popular in Scotland, probably due to the lead singer and songwriter with Marillion being a Scotsman known as Fish (real name Derek Dick from Dalkeith in Midlothian). Fish has said that the name Kayleigh was an amalgamation of different women's names, but the name did exist before 1985, either as a variation of the girls' name Kaylee or as the anglicized form of the Gaelic word *ceilidh* meaning 'a Scottish dance or gathering'.

Keir

Scottish surname that is generally considered to be a variation of the surname Kerr, although there are also places called Keir in Stirling and Dumfries and Galloway. The name Kerr either derives from the Gaelic word *carr* meaning 'fort', the Gaelic word *ciar* meaning 'dusky', or the Norse and Old English word *carr* meaning 'marsh'. Famous Keirs include Scottish socialist and founder of the British Labour Party, Keir Hardie.

Keith

Surname and popular boys' first name. The name comes from the town of Keith in Moray. The town derives its name either from the Pictish first name *Cait* or from the Brythonic word *coit* meaning 'wood'. Famous Keiths include Penelope Keith, star of the television comedy *The Good Life*, television presenter Keith 'Cheggers' Chegwin, drummer Keith Moon from The Who, and guitarist Keith Richards from The Rolling Stones, who is affectionately known as 'Keef'.

Kelly

Surname and both male and female first name. It is the most common surname in Scotland of recent Irish origin. Kelly is the second most common surname in Ireland and derives from the Irish first name *Ceallagh*, which is of uncertain origin but possibly means 'strife' or 'church'. Famous Scottish Kellys include the irrepressibly perky GMTV presenter Lorraine Kelly and singer Kelly Marie who got to number one with the irrepressibly catchy 'Feels Like I'm in Love' in 1980.

Kennedy

Surname and occasional male first name. The name originated in Ireland and became established in Ayrshire in the 13th century before being taken back to Northern Ireland and around the word. The name derives from the Gaelic *ceann eidigh* meaning 'ugly head'. Famous Scottish Kennedys include broadcaster Ludovic Kennedy and Liberal leader Charles Kennedy, neither of whom could be said to have especially ugly heads. The American political dynasty of Kennedys originates from the Irish Kennedys.

Kenneth

Male first name. The name is the anglicized form of a Gaelic first name *Cinaed* and Pictish first name *Ciniod*, both meaning 'born of fire' and another Gaelic first name *Coinnich* or *Coinneach* meaning 'handsome' or 'fair'. Three of Scotland's earliest kings were called Kenneth including Kenneth MacAlpine who in 843 united the kingdoms of the Scots and the Picts. Diminutives of the name include Ken and Kenny.

Other famous Kenneths include the author of *The Wind in the Willows*, Kenneth Grahame, first President of Zambia Kenneth Kaunda, Scottish footballer Kenny Dalglish, Conservative politician Kenneth Clarke, comic actor Kenneth Williams, and former Mayor of London Ken Livingstone. Ken Hutchinson was the full name of Hutch from television series *Starsky and Hutch*, and Ken Barlow is a character who has featured in *Coronation Street* from its very first episode in 1960. One year later, in 1961, a slightly different Ken was introduced as the boyfriend of popular Mattel toy doll Barbie, and the couple have been going steady ever since.

Kenny McCormick is the name of a character from the cult television series *South Park*. He would end up dead in every single episode of the show's first five series, resulting in the catch-phrase 'Oh my God, they killed Kenny!'

Kenzie

Male first name that derives from the Scottish surname MacKenzie meaning 'son of Kenneth'. The recent popularity as a first name might be associated with Kenzie, rapper with Blazin' Squad and runner-up in *Celebrity Big Brother*, whose real name is James MacKenzie.

Kerr, Carr

Scottish surname from the Borders and occasional male first name. The name either derives from the Gaelic word *carr* meaning 'fort', the Gaelic word *ciar* meaning 'dusky' or the Norse and Old English word *carr* meaning 'marsh'. The surname Carr can be a variation of Kerr. Famous Scottish Kerrs include lead singer of Simple Minds Jim Kerr and Hollywood film star Deborah Kerr, best known for *From Here to Eternity*, who to confuse matters pronounces her surname 'carr' rather than 'kerr'.

Kidd

Surname that in Scotland derives from the first name Kid. This was a diminutive of Christopher, which comes from the Greek *Khristophoros* meaning 'bearer of Christ' and made popular by Saint Christopher, the patron saint of travellers. Famous Kidds include model Jodie Kidd and Scottish sea captain William Kidd, who was executed for piracy in 1701 and whose treasure has never been found.

Kirk

Scottish male first name and surname. The name is derived from the Scots word *kirk* meaning 'church', with particular reference to the Presbyterian Church of Scotland. The Scots word originally comes from the Greek *kyriakon* meaning 'Lord's house', and was brought to Scotland through the Norse variation *kirke*. Famous Kirks include Hollywood film star Kirk Douglas and captain of the *Starship Enterprise* James

T. Kirk, whose name could not be more Scottish were it not for the fact that the T stands for 'Tiberius'.

Kirkpatrick

Scottish surname that originated from two villages in Dumfries and Galloway called Kirkpatrick and means 'church of St Patrick'. Famous Kirkpatricks include the Scotsman credited with inventing the bicycle, Kirkpatrick Macmillan.

Kirsty, Kirstie

Female first name that was originally a diminutive of Kirstin or Kirsten. These were Scottish and Scandinavian variations of Christine and Christina, the feminine forms of the name Christian. Famous Kirstys include singer Kirsty MacColl and Scottish broadcasters Kirsty Wark and Kirsty Young. Famous Kirsties include American actress Kirstie Alley and *Location, Location, Location* presenter Kirstie Allsopp.

Knox

Scottish surname that originated in Renfrewshire. The name is derived from the Gaelic *cnoc* meaning 'hill' or 'hillock'. Scotland's most famous Knox is Protestant reformer John Knox. Other famous Knoxes include Barbara Knox, who has played Rita in *Coronation Street* for over 35 years, the Fort Knox gold-bullion depository in Fort Knox, Kentucky, and Knox Jolie-Pitt, the son of Angelina and Brad.

Kyle

Scottish surname that has recently become a popular male first name. Kyle comes from the Gaelic word *caol* meaning either 'strait' or else 'person who lives at the strait'. There are several geographic Kyles in Scotland, the most famous being the Ayrshire district of Kyle and the Highland village of Kyle of Lochalsh at the mainland end of the Skye Bridge. Famous Kyles have included *Twin Peaks* and *Desperate Housewives* star Kyle MacLachlan and mainstay of daytime television Jeremy Kyle. Selina Kyle is the alter ego of Batman's sometime adversary Catwoman.

Lachlan

Male first name that derives from the Gaelic *lochlann* meaning 'land of the lochs'. The name traditionally referred to a person who came from Norway. Famous Lachlans include Lachlan Macquarie, the 18th-century Governor of New South Wales who is sometimes given the name of 'the Father of Australia'. His influence resulted in Lachlan becoming a popular Australian first name, and the Lachlan River in New South Wales is named after him.

Laird

Scottish surname that comes from the Scots word *laird* meaning 'landowner'. John Laird was a Scottish shipbuilder who founded the company that is now known as Cammell Laird.

Lamont

Scottish surname that originated in Argyll. The name is derived from the Norse *log mann* meaning 'lawman' or 'lawgiver'. Famous Scottish Lamonts include former Chancellor of the Exchequer Norman Lamont, who did not stress the first syllable of his surname in the Scottish manner, but followed the Anglo-French manner by stressing the second syllable. The availability of two pronunciations for the name has led to considerable confusion, with the rugby-playing brothers Sean and Rory Lamont having their surnames pronounced differently in turn, often by the same commentator in the same game.

Laurie, Lawrie

Scottish surname that derives from the diminutive forms of the male first name Laurence or Lawrence. The first name in turn derives from the Latin name *Laurentius*, which originally referred to inhabitants of the ancient Italian town of Laurentum and became a popular male first name after the 3rd-century Christian martyr Saint Laurence.

Famous Lauries include English actor Hugh Laurie and Scottish actor John Laurie, who played Private Frazer in *Dad's Army*. Famous Lawries include Scottish golfer Paul Lawrie, who won the 1999 Open Championship, and Scottish singer Marie Lawrie (who is better known to both Take That and the general public as Lulu).

Law

Surname that derives from the Scots word *law* meaning 'hill'. People with this surname are not, therefore, descended from lawyers or solicitors but from people who lived on a hill. Famous Laws include footballer Denis Law and Conservative politician Andrew Bonar Law, who may have been born in Canada but came from a Scottish family and was brought up in Glasgow before eventually becoming British Prime Minister in 1922.

Lawson

Predominantly Scottish surname. It may derive from the surname Law (meaning 'dweller on the hill') or from the male first name Lawrence (meaning 'man from the town of Laurentum'). Famous Lawsons include Scottish actor Denis Lawson, who starred in *Local Hero*, and Conservative politician Nigel Lawson and his celebrity daughter Nigella, whose family were originally Latvian and changed their name from Leibson to Lawson on arriving in Britain.

Leask

Scottish surname that has become established in Shetland. It is thought that the name originated in a place in Aberdeenshire formerly called Leask (now Pitlurg), before moving north. It has also been suggested (although not widely accepted) that the name might be derived from the Gaelic *lasgair* meaning 'brave'.

Lennox

Surname that takes its name from the historic region of Lennox that would become Dunbartonshire. The name is Brythonic in origin and possibly means 'men of the Leven', in reference to the River Leven that flows from Loch Lomond to Dumbarton. Lennox would become first a powerful earldom in the 13th century and then the title of dukedom in 1581. Famous Lennoxes include Scottish singer Annie Lennox and the English–Canadian world heavyweight boxing champion with the very Scottish name of Lennox Lewis.

Leslie, Lesley

Scottish surname and both male and female first name. The name originates from the village called Leslie in Aberdeenshire, which is derived from the Gaelic *lios laith* (with *lios* meaning 'enclosure' or 'garden' and *liath* meaning 'grey') or *lios linn* (with *linn* meaning 'pool'). Therefore Leslie could either be 'grey enclosure' or the slightly nicer 'garden pool'. The Leslies moved to Fife in the 13th century, and the Fife town of Leslie is named after the family. The Leslies became known as a family of soldiers and led the armies of the Scottish Covenanters in the 17th century.

Famous Leslies include the English film actor Leslie Howard, who starred in *Gone with the Wind*, Canadian film actor Leslie Nielsen who starred in *Airplane* and *The Naked Gun*, and Leslie Townes Hope who is better known as Bob Hope.

Lesley has become the more common female version of the name and famous Lesleys include opera singer Lesley Garrett and English model Lesley Hornby, who is better known as Twiggy.

Lewis

Currently the most popular boys' name in Scotland. Although Lewis is also an English first name – a variation of the French *Louis* – and a common Welsh and English surname (as in the name of Inspector Morse's Geordie sidekick), most Scottish Lewises are named after the Hebridean Isle of Lewis.

Lewis is in fact only the northern part of the Hebridean island (with Harris being the southern part), and the name probably derives from the Norse *ljodhus* meaning 'homes of the people', as Lewis was ruled for centuries by Scandinavians. Gaelic is spoken in most of the island and the Gaelic name for Lewis is *Leodhais*. It is often said that the Gaelic version of the name is derived from *leoghuis* meaning 'marshy'.

Famous Scots called Lewis include the author of *Sunset Song*, Lewis Grassic Gibbon. Formula One motor-racing star Lewis Hamilton does not have any immediate Scottish ancestry but his name is somewhat remarkably composed of two well-known Scottish place names.

Liddell

Surname that derives from the Liddle Water, a river in the Borders. Famous Liddells include Olympic champion Eric Liddell, whose life story was told in

Chariots of Fire, and Alice Liddell, the young girl who was the inspiration for Alice in Lewis Carroll's *Alice's Adventures in Wonderland*. The discount supermarket chain Lidl is not connected to the surname, but originated in Germany.

Lindsay

Surname, male first name and female first name associated with Scotland. The name comes from the Norman family of de Limesay, which originated in Limesay in Normandy, but came to Scotland via the region of Lindsey in the English county of Lincolnshire. Limesay means 'island of lime-trees'. Famous Lindsays include British actor Robert Lindsay and American actresses Lindsay Lohan and the original bionic woman, Lindsay Wagner.

Livingstone

Surname that is derived from the differently spelled Livingston in West Lothian (where there was a settlement long before the current new town). The place was named after either an English landowner called Leving or a Flemish merchant called De Leving who settled there in the 12th century. Famous Livingstones include Scottish missionary and explorer David Livingstone and former Mayor of London Ken Livingstone (who is of Scottish descent, we presume).

Lockhart

Scottish surname that originated in Dumfries and Galloway. The name does not, as you might imagine, derive from the word 'loch', but instead appears to derive from a family or person called *Locard*, who was either Norman or Scandinavian. The name *Locard* is of Germanic origin with *loc* meaning 'lock' and *ard* meaning 'hardy' or 'brave'. Famous Lockharts include Gilderoy Lockhart, teacher at Hogwarts School of Witchcraft and Wizardry in *Harry Potter and the Chamber of Secrets*.

The Locard family would also give their name to the Dumfries and Galloway town of Lockerbie.

Logan

Scottish surname and both male and female first name. The name comes from the Gaelic word *lagan* meaning 'little hollow' and was also a place name in Ayrshire.

Famous Logans include Logan International Airport in Boston, Johnny Logan, who was twice winner of the Eurovision Song Contest, and the 1976 science-fiction film *Logan's Run*. Logan is also the other name of *X-Men* character Wolverine, and the loganberry was named after a judge called James Harvey Logan who crossed a raspberry and a blackberry. Mount

Logan is the highest peak in Canada and was named after Canadian geologist William Logan.

Lorna

Female first name associated with Scotland since the novel *Lorna Doone* by R.D. Blackmore was published in 1869. Although Blackmore was English and the book was set in Exmoor in Devon, it is said that the heroine Lorna was named after the Lorne district in Argyll, and the name Lorna became popular in Scotland.

The place name Lorne derives from the name *Lorn*, one of the early rulers of the kingdom of Dalriada who came to Scotland from Ireland in the 5th century.

Lorne

Surname and male first name that comes (like Lorna) from the Argyll district of Lorne. This became especially popular as a first name in Canada. Famous Lornes include Lorne Greene, Canadian star of *Bonanza* and *Battlestar Galactica*, and Scottish comedian Tommy Lorne, who is credited with inventing the popular Scottish breakfast delicacy of the square-shaped Lorne sausage.

Lyle

Surname and male first name that is derived from the French *l'isle* meaning 'the island'. Famous Scottish Lyles include golfer Sandy Lyle and Abram Lyle, a sugar refiner from Greenock who became known for Lyle's golden syrup and whose company would later become part of Tate & Lyle.

MacAdam

Scottish surname that originated in Ayrshire. The name means 'son of Adam', with Adam being the name of the first man in the Bible and believed to mean simply 'man' in Hebrew. Famous MacAdams include engineer John Loudon MacAdam, who invented the technique of using uniform small stones to construct road surfaces that would bear his name. When tar was later added to the mixture, the process would be called 'tar macadam' in his honour.

Famous Scots called Adam include Adam Smith, who is known as 'the father of economics', and the Adam family that included brothers John, James, and Robert Adam, who were Britain's leading architects in the 18th century. The Addams family of the 20th-century television series does not (as far as we know) have any connection with Scotland.

MacAlister, MacAllister

Scottish surname and clan that became established in Kintyre and Bute. The name MacAlister means 'son of Alexander' or 'son of Alistair' with Alexander meaning 'defender of men' and Alistair and Alasdair being its Scottish and Gaelic variants. The first chief of the Clan MacAlister was Alexander, a descendant of the famous Somerled, King of the Isles.

There are many different spellings of the name, and famous people with the surname include Scottish footballer Gary McAllister and Kevin McCallister, the character played by Macaulay Culkin in *Home Alone*.

MacAlpine, McAlpine

Historic Scottish surname. The name originated with Kenneth, son of Alpin, who in 843 became King of both Picts and Scots, and in the process began a royal dynasty that would rule the new kingdom of Alba until the death of Malcolm II in 1034. Little is known about Kenneth MacAlpine himself, even whether he was a Scot or a Pict, and the origin of the name Alpin is obscure, but it is thought to be of Pictish or Brythonic derivation, coming from the word *alp* meaning 'rock' (also responsible for the name of the European mountain range the Alps). It is thought that *alp* derives from the Latin word *albus* meaning 'white', although it is possible that the Latin word might itself derive from an even earlier Celtic word.

The MacAlpines became established in Perthshire, and famous McAlpines include Scottish builder Robert McAlpine, who founded one of the biggest construction companies in the world and gained the nickname of 'Concrete Bob'.

MacAndrew, McAndrew

Scottish surname that means 'son of Andrew'. Andrew is the patron saint of Scotland (as well as Greece and Russia). Famous McAndrews include model Nell McAndrew.

MacArthur

Scottish surname and clan that became established in the Lorne district of Argyll. The name MacArthur means 'son of Arthur', with the name believed to derive from the Old Gaelic word *art* for 'bear' and Arthur becoming the anglicized form of the Gaelic name *Artair* meaning 'bear-like'. Arthur is, of course, also associated with the legendary Celtic king of the Britons who lived in Camelot and presided over the Knights of the Round Table.

Famous Scottish Arthurs included British Prime

Minister Arthur Balfour and the creator of Sherlock Holmes, Arthur Conan Doyle. Famous MacArthurs include American general Douglas MacArthur, who commanded the Allied forces in the Pacific in the Second World War, yachtswoman Ellen MacArthur, and 'MacArthur Park', a hit song for Richard Harris and Donna Summer, which was named after a park in Los Angeles.

MacAskill, McCaskill

Scottish surname that originated in Lewis and Skye. The name comes from the Gaelic *MacAsgaill*, derived in turn from the Norse name *Askell* or *Asketil* meaning 'cauldron of sacrifice to the gods'. Famous MacAskills include Scottish Justice Minister Kenny MacAskill and smiley-faced Scottish weatherman Ian McCaskill.

MacAulay, Macaulay

Scottish surname that originated in Lewis, although there are also MacAulays from Dunbartonshire. In most cases the name comes from the Gaelic *MacAmhlaidh* meaning 'son of Amhlaoibh', with Aulay being the anglicized form of *Amhlaoibh*, which is in turn the Gaelic variant of the Norse name Olaf meaning 'ancestor's descendant'. Famous Macaulays include Sarah Macaulay, the wife of Prime Minister

Gordon Brown, Scottish comedian Fred MacAulay, and American child star Macaulay Culkin.

MacBeth, Macbeth

Name of possibly Scotland's most famous monarch. Macbeth, who ruled as king from 1040 to 1057, is forever associated with the historically inaccurate but world-renowned play *Macbeth* by William Shakespeare. The play was written in the 1600s and is known in the theatrical world as 'the Scottish play'. In reality Macbeth was Thane of Moray (and not Glamis or Cawdor) and the Macbeths were an established family in the north of Scotland, with the name meaning 'son of life' or 'son of a man of religion'. Other famous MacBeths include the hero of the Scottish television series *Hamish MacBeth*. The real name of Lady Macbeth was Gruoch, which has strangely not yet caught on as a first name.

MacCallum, McCallum

Scottish surname that is a variation of Malcolm. It is the anglicized form of the Gaelic *Mac Gille Chalium* and means 'son of the servant of Columba', with *Columba* being the Latin form of the Irish *Colm* meaning 'dove'. Saint Columba was an Irish missionary who founded a monastery on Iona.

Famous MacCallums include Scottish actor David McCallum, who starred in *The Man from UNCLE*.

MacCartney, McCartney

Scottish surname that originates in Galloway. The name means 'son of Art' with *Art* the Gaelic for 'bear'. Famous McCartneys include the Beatle Paul McCartney, who lived for a time not far from Galloway in Kintyre, and his fashion-designer daughter Stella McCartney, who was married on the Isle of Bute.

McClintock, McLintock, MacLintock

Scottish surname that derives from the Gaelic *Mac Gille Fhiondaig* and means 'son of the servant of Saint Findon'. Saint Findon is believed to have been a 7th-century disciple of Saint Columba, and the name Findon derives from the Gaelic *fionn* meaning 'fair'. The MacLintocks became established around Loch Lomond and famous McLintocks include footballer Frank McLintock, captain of the Arsenal double-winning team of 1971, and a 1963 John Wayne western called *McLintock!*

MacColl, McColl

Scottish surname that originated in Argyll. The name comes from the surname MacColla and means 'son of Colla', with *Colla* being an old Gaelic first name that possibly means 'high one'. Alasdair MacColla was the Highland leader of the Royalist forces in the Civil Wars of the 1640s and Robert McColl was the name of the Scottish footballer who founded the R.S. McColl chain of newsagents. Other famous MacColls include songwriter Ewan MacColl and his daughter Kirsty MacColl. Kirsty had her greatest success singing with The Pogues on 'A Fairytale of New York', and another of The Pogues most popular songs was 'Dirty Old Town', which was written by her father.

MacConnell, McConnell

Scottish surname. The name does not (as you might imagine) derive from the Irish surname Connel, but instead, as with the surname MacDonnell, is a variation of the surname MacDonald meaning 'son of Donald', or its Gaelic form *Mac Dhomhnuill*. Famous McConnells include Scotland's third First Minister, Jack McConnell.

MacDiarmid, McDiarmid

Scottish surname that derives from the Gaelic *Mac Dhiarmaid* and means 'son of Dermott'. *Diarmaid* a Gaelic and Irish first name meaning 'freeman' or 'free from envy', and Dermott is the anglicized form of the name. The MacDiarmids originated in Perthshire and famous MacDiarmids include Scottish poet Hugh MacDiarmid (whose real name was Christopher Grieve) and Scottish actor Ian McDiarmid, who played the Emperor and the Dark Lord of the Sith in the *Star Wars* films. McDiarmid Park is also the name of St Johnstone Football Club's ground in Perth. The stadium is fully floodlit, and so it is very unusual for the ground to have a 'dark side'.

MacDonald, McDonald, Macdonald

The most common surname in Scotland beginning with 'Mac'. In Gaelic, *mac* means 'son of' and so MacDonald means 'son of Donald'. Donald is a name of Gaelic origin that means 'world ruler' and MacDonald is the anglicized form of the Gaelic *Mac Dhomhnuill*.

MacDonald is currently the 9th most common surname in Scotland, but if you were to add all those with the spelling 'McDonald' it would be the fourth most common surname.

The MacDonalds took their name from a Donald who was the son of the legendary 12th-century Hebridean warlord Somerled. The family would dominate the Hebrides in the 13th to 15th centuries from their island stronghold of Islay, holding the title of Lord of the Isles. Further north, the MacDonalds of Clanranald were pre-eminent in the northern Hebrides. Other MacDonalds were established at Sleat in Skye, in Ardnamurchan, and in Glencoe, where in February 1692 the famous massacre took place with 38 MacDonalds being killed in very cold blood by a Government regiment led by Campbells.

Famous MacDonalds include Jacobite heroine Flora MacDonald, Britain's first Labour Prime Minister James Ramsay MacDonald, the first ever Prime Minister of Canada John MacDonald, and newsreader Trevor McDonald.

The first McDonald's fast-food restaurant was opened by two McDonald brothers in California in 1940 and McDonald's (with the clown Ronald McDonald leading their marketing campaign) would eventually become the world's largest chain of restaurants, serving over 40 million customers a day – so the definition of MacDonald as 'world ruler' certainly proved to be true in this case.

An elderly MacDonald also gives his name to the famous children's song 'Old MacDonald Had a Farm', and on the farm you will usually find a duck, a cow, a dog, and a pig, although some versions have other livestock. The ee-eye-ee-eye-oh part remains constant, however.

MacDonnell

Scottish surname and clan that became established on the Scottish mainland in Glengarry in the Highlands and Keppoch in Lochaber. The name derived from the clan name MacDonald meaning 'son of Donald'. Famous MacDonnells include American aviation pioneer James Smith McDonnell, who would merge his company with another American aviation company of Scottish descent to form aircraft manufacturers MacDonnell-Douglas.

MacDougall, MacDougal, McDougall

Scottish surname and clan that became established in the Lorne region of Argyll. As with the Clan MacDonald, the MacDougalls were descended from the legendary warlord Somerled, in this case from his son Dougal. The name MacDougall derives from the Gaelic *MacDhugaill* and means 'son of Dougal', with Dougal meaning 'dark stranger'. Famous MacDougalls include Islay born Alexander McDougall, who became both a leader in the American War of Independence and a New York banker and had the famous MacDougal Street in Greenwich Village named after him.

MacDuff

Scottish surname that means 'son of Duff'. The name Duff comes from the Gaelic *duibh* meaning 'black'. The MacDuffs were the famous Thanes of Fife who helped Malcolm Canmore regain the throne from Macbeth in 1057. MacDuff is forever remembered from the line from William Shakespeare's *Macbeth* which is often misquoted as 'Lead on, MacDuff'. The actual line spoken by Macbeth is 'Lay on, MacDuff', inviting the would-be avenger to attack him in the belief that no 'man of woman born' could kill him. MacDuff was able to kill Macbeth however as he was not 'a man of woman born', but born by Caesarean section.

The Duffs would later become the Earls of Fife and built both the town of MacDuff on the north-east coast and in 1817 also the town of Dufftown in Moray, later to become one of the most famous centres of the malt-whisky industry.

MacEwan, McEwan, MacEwen

Scottish surname that means 'son of Ewan'. Ewan is a version of the Gaelic name *Eoghan*, which is of obscure origin, but might possibly mean 'of the yew tree' or 'of youth'. Famous MacEwans include author Ian McEwan, actress Geraldine McEwan, and Scottish brewer William McEwan, who founded the Fountain Brewery in Edinburgh, best known for producing McEwan's Export in its famous red tins with the logo of a laughing Cavalier.

MacFadyen, McFadden

Surname that is the anglicized form of the Gaelic *Mac Phaiden* meaning 'son of little Patrick'. The MacFadyens were Irish in origin before settling in Mull in the 14th century. There are several variations of MacFadyen, the most common being McFadden. Famous MacFadyens include actors Matthew MacFadyen and Angus MacFadyen, who played Robert the Bruce in *Braveheart*. Famous McFaddens include Scottish footballer James McFadden, actor Steve McFadden, who plays Phil Mitchell in *EastEnders*, and the title character of the cartoon *Caspar the Friendly Ghost*, whose full name is actually Caspar McFadden.

MacFarlane, Macfarlane

Scottish surname and Loch Lomond clan from the 13th century. The name means 'son of Parlan' with *Parlan* being the Gaelic for Bartholomew, the name of one of Jesus' disciples, which in Aramaic means 'son of Talmai', with *Talmai* meaning 'farmer'.

MacFie, McPhee

Scottish surname that became established on the small Hebridean island of Colonsay and is the anglicized form of *Mac Duibshithe* meaning 'son of Dubshithe'. *Duibshithe* is an old Gaelic personal name that means 'dark peace'. Famous McPhees include the heroine of *Nanny McPhee*, the 2005 film starring Emma Thompson.

MacGill, McGill

Scottish surname that originated in Dumfries and Galloway. The name comes from the Gaelic *Mac an Ghoill* and means 'son of the stranger' (referring to an incomer to the area). Famous McGills include McGill University in Montreal, Canada, and saucy English postcard artist Donald McGill.

MacGowan, McGowan

Surname that derives from the Gaelic *Mac Ghobhainn* and means 'son of the smith' (the smith in question being a metalworker, such as a blacksmith or silversmith). Famous MacGowans include impressionist Alistair McGowan and indestructible Pogues singer Shane MacGowan.

MacGregor, McGregor, Macgregor

Scottish surname meaning 'son of Gregor'. Gregor was the Scottish form of Gregory, a name that comes from the Greek meaning 'watchful' and was a popular name for popes. Another theory is that the name originates with a 9th-century Scottish prince called Gregor. The MacGregors were concentrated between Aberfoyle and Balquhidder in the Trossachs, and were involved in decades of conflict with the Campbells and the Scottish Crown. This ultimately led to them being dispossessed of their lands, and the entire clan was outlawed from 1603 until 1774. This period of non-existence saw the MacGregors called 'The Children of the Mist'.

Famous MacGregors include 'Rob Roy' Macgregor, who was a real-life outlaw and the hero of a work of a fiction by Sir Walter Scott, Radio 4 presenter Sue MacGregor, and Scottish film star Ewan McGregor.

MacIan, McKean

Scottish surname that means 'son of Iain' or 'son of John'. The Clan MacIan became established in Ardnamurchan. Anglicized variations of MacIan included McKean and Caine. This latter form would become the stage name of a certain young English actor called Maurice Micklewhite when his original choice of 'Michael Scott' had been ruled out –

another actor already had the name – and he decided that 'Michael Caine' would do instead.

The surname McCain, as in American presidential candidate John McCain, also derives from MacIan, but you may be glad to hear it is an Irish rather than a Scottish variation.

MacInnes

Scottish surname and clan that means 'son of Angus'. The name derives from *Aonghus*, the Gaelic form of the name Angus, which is pronounced 'Innes'. The surname MacInnes is not connected to the surname Innes (which comes from the Gaelic *inis* meaning 'small island'). The MacInneses were found on the west coast and in Perthshire, and famous people called MacInnes include mountaineer Hamish MacInnes.

MacIntosh, Mackintosh, Macintosh

Scottish surname and clan from Perthshire and the Highlands. The name comes from the Gaelic *mac an toisich* meaning 'son of the chieftain', with the Scottish Gaelic *toisich* being similar to the Irish word *taoiseach* that is the title of the Irish Prime Minister. Famous MacIntoshes include Scottish architect and designer Charles Rennie Mackintosh, the waterproof jacket that was invented by Scot Charles Macintosh in 1823, and the Apple Macintosh personal computer, often abbreviated to just 'Mac', that was launched in 1984 and is possibly the most famous computer in the world.

MacIntyre, McIntyre, Macintyre

Scottish surname and clan from Glencoe. The name comes from the Gaelic *mac an t-saoir* meaning 'son of the carpenter'. MacIntyre is often anglicized to the surname Wright. MacIntyre was the name of the character played by Peter Riegert in the film *Local Hero*, who was chosen by oil boss Burt Lancaster to go to Scotland to buy out the local villagers on the basis of his Scottish surname, not realizing that his family actually came from Hungary.

MacIver, MacIvor

Scottish surname that became established in Argyll. The name comes from the Gaelic *Mac Iomhairr* meaning 'son of Ivor', with Ivor being a popular male first name that derives from the Scandinavian *Ivarr* meaning 'bow' and 'army'.

MacKay, Mackay, McCoy, MacKie, Mackie

Scottish surname meaning 'son of Aodh' or 'son of Aed'. The Gaelic name *Aodh* means 'fire', and would be anglicized as Hugh. The MacKays were found throughout Scotland, but became established in Sutherland. The Highland Clearances of the 19th century saw many MacKays scattered around the world. Famous MacKays include Scottish footballer Dave Mackay, Orcadian writer George Mackay Brown, and blended whisky Whyte and Mackay.

Mackay is also a coastal town of 90,000 people in Queensland, Australia, named after Scottish explorer John Mackay.

The phrase 'the real McCoy', used when talking about something that is 'the genuine article' is of uncertain origin. However, it is likely to be a variation of the surname Mackay, and the phrase 'the real Mackay' was used in the 19th century in Scotland to promote whisky. Famous McCoys include Scottish actor Sylvester McCoy, who played Doctor Who, and another doctor, Leonard McCoy, who was affectionately known as 'Bones' in *Star Trek*. Rather worryingly for a medical practitioner, he was best known for the catch-phrase 'He's dead, Jim.'

The surnames MacKie and Mackie are also variations of Mackay.

MacKenzie, McKenzie, Mackenzie

Scottish surname that means 'son of Kenneth'. It is the anglicized version of the Gaelic *Mac Coinnich* meaning 'son of Coinnich'. Kenneth means 'handsome' or 'fair' and was the name of three of Scotland's earliest kings.

The MacKenzies were concentrated in Wester Ross. Famous MacKenzies include Scottish explorer Alexander Mackenzie, who had Canada's longest river named after him, Canadian Prime Minister William Lyon Mackenzie King, writer Compton Mackenzie, the author of *Whisky Galore*, singer Scott McKenzie, who in 1967 got to number one with 'San Francisco (Be Sure to Wear Flowers in Your Hair)', and Mackenzie Crook, who played Gareth in the television series *The Office*.

MacKinlay, McKinley

Scottish surname that originated chiefly in Perthshire. The name means 'son of Finlay' and is the anglicized form of *Mac Fhionnlaigh* with Finlay meaning 'fair warrior'. Famous MacKinlays include American President William McKinley, who was assassinated in 1901 and gave his name to Mount McKinley in Alaska, which at over 20,000 feet is the highest peak in North America.

McKinney

Scottish surname that is a variation of the predominantly Irish surname McKenna. The name means 'son of Cionadh' with the Gaelic name *Cionadh* meaning 'beloved of Aodh' (Aodh being the Celtic god of fire). McKinney is a city in Texas with a population of over 100,000.

MacKinnon

Scottish surname that originated chiefly in Mull and Iona. The name means 'son of Fingon' and is the anglicized form of *Mac Fhionghuin*, with Fingon being a descendant of Kenneth MacAlpine whose name means 'fair born'.

MacLachlan

Scottish surname that is the anglicized form of *Mac Lachlainn* meaning 'son of Lachlan'. The name Lachlan comes from the Gaelic name *Lochlann* meaning 'land of the lochs' and historically referred to a person who came from Norway. Famous MacLachlans include the American actor Kyle MacLachlan who starred in *Twin Peaks*, *Desperate Housewives* and *Sex and the City*.

MacLaren, McLaren

Scottish surname that originated chiefly in
Perthshire. The name means 'son of Laurence' and
is the anglicized form of the Gaelic *Mac Labhruinn*.
The male first name Laurence or Lawrence derives
from the Latin *Laurentius* referring to a person from
the ancient Italian town of Laurentum. It became
a popular male first name after the 3rd-century
Christian martyr Saint Laurence.

Famous MacLarens include Malcolm McLaren,
the manager of The Sex Pistols, Scottish rugby
commentator Bill McLaren, and short-lived England
football manager Steve McLaren. Bruce McLaren
was the New Zealand motor-racing driver who in
1963 founded the McLaren Formula One racing
team, which has had many world champion drivers
including Nikki Lauda, Alain Prost, Ayrton Senna
and the very Scottish sounding, but not Scottish,
Lewis Hamilton.

MacLean, McLean, MacLaine

Scottish surname that means 'son of the follower
of St John'. The name is the anglicized form of the
Gaelic *MacGille Eoinoinnich*. The founder of the
clan was called 'Gillean of the battle-axe' and the
MacLeans became concentrated in Mull and Tiree.
Famous MacLeans include British spy Donald

Maclean and American singer of 'American Pie'
Don McLean. Famous Scottish MacLeans include
Gaelic poet Sorley MacLean, radical political leader
John MacLean, Dundee United football manager
Jim McLean, and best-selling thriller writer Alistair
MacLean.

The surname MacLaine is a variation of MacLean
and originated in Mull. Famous MacLaines include
Shirley MacLaine, the American film star, and John
McClane, the character played by Bruce Willis in the
Die Hard films.

McLeish

Scottish surname that derives from the Gaelic *Mac
Gille Iosa* meaning 'son of the servant of Jesus'. It is
a variation on the Scottish surname Gillies. Famous
McLeishes include football manager Alex McLeish
and the second First Minister of Scotland, Henry
McLeish.

MacLennan, McLennan

Scottish surname that is the anglicized form of the
Gaelic *Mac Fhinneain* and means 'son of the servant
of Saint Finnan'. Saint Finnan was a 7th-century Irish
saint whose name is derived from the Gaelic name
Fionn meaning 'white'.

MacLeod, McLeod, McCloud

Scottish surname that means 'son of Leod'. The name Leod derives from the Norse word *ljotr* and unfortunately means 'ugly'. The Clan MacLeod was concentrated in Skye and Lewis.

Famous MacLeods include Scottish football manager Ally MacLeod and Connor MacLeod, the immortal hero of the *Highlander* films. The American surname McCloud, familiar as the title of a 1970s television show, is a variation of MacLeod.

MacMillan, McMillan, Macmillan

Scottish surname that derives from the Gaelic *mac mhaolain* or *MacGille Mhaoil* meaning 'son of the tonsured one'. The name is therefore believed to originate from monks. The MacMillans became established in first Argyll and then Kintyre and Galloway. Famous MacMillans include Scottish inventor of the bicycle Kirkpatrick Macmillan, Daniel Macmillan from Arran, who founded the international publishing company of Macmillan, and his grandson Harold Macmillan, who became British Prime Minister and was nicknamed 'Supermac'. The name was also used for the characters played by Rock Hudson and Susan Saint James in the television series *McMillan and Wife*.

MacNab, McNab

Scottish surname that is the anglicized form of
the Gaelic *Mac an Aba*, which means 'son of the
abbot' or 'father's son'. The MacNab family became
established near Killin. Andy McNab is the author of
Bravo Two Zero, while *John Macnab* is the title of a
novel by John Buchan.

MacNeill, McNeill

Scottish surname that means 'son of Neil'. The name
comes from the Gaelic *Mac Niall* meaning 'son of
Niall', with Neil or Niall meaning 'champion'. The
name is long associated with the island of Barra,
where it is said that the name originated from an
Irishman called Niall who settled there in the 11th
century. Famous MacNeills include American artist
James McNeill Whistler and Billy McNeill, captain
of Celtic's European Cup winning team of 1967.

MacPhail, McFall

Scottish surname derived from the Gaelic name
Mac Phail. The name means 'son of Paul', with
Paul being a popular male first name derived from
the Latin name *Paulus* meaning 'small'. It was
popularized through Saint Paul, who was converted
to Christianity on the road to Damascus and was

instrumental in founding the Christian church. The surname McFall is a variation of MacPhail.

MacPherson, Macpherson

Scottish surname that means 'son of a parson'. Famous MacPhersons include the Scottish poet of *Ossian* James Macpherson, Scottish football commentator Archie MacPherson, and Australian model Elle MacPherson. It seems unlikely, however, that Archie and Elle are closely related.

Macquarrie

Scottish surname from the island of Mull. The name comes from the Gaelic *Mac Guaidhre* meaning 'son of a proud man'. Famous Macquarries include Lachlan Macquarie from the small island of Ulva, near Mull, who was Governor General of New South Wales in the early 19th century and is often called 'the Father of Australia'. Numerous place names and institutions in Australia are called Macquarie after him.

MacQueen, McQueen

Scottish surname that does not have any connection with any Scottish queen. It is an anglicized variation of the Argyll surname MacSween, which either means 'son of Suibne' (with *Suibne* the Gaelic for 'pleasant') or 'son of Sweyn' (with *Sweyn* a Norse name meaning 'servant'). Famous McQueens include fashion designer Alexander McQueen and film star Steve McQueen.

MacRae, McCrae

Scottish surname that became established in Wester Ross. The name is the anglicized form of the Gaelic *Mac Rath* and means 'son of grace'. Famous MacRaes include American star of *Oklahoma* Gordon MacRae, Scottish world rally champion Colin McRae, and singer George McCrae who had a number one hit with 'Rock Your Baby'.

MacTaggart

Scottish surname that is derived from the Gaelic name *Mac an-T-Saigart* and means 'son of the priest'. The name comes from the days when priests were allowed to acknowledge their children. MacTaggarts were first found in Ross and in Dumfries, and famous MacTaggarts include the two Scottish painters called William MacTaggart.

The surname Taggart is a common variant of this name.

MacTavish, McTavish

Scottish surname that is derived from the Gaelic name *Mac Tamhais*. The name means 'son of Thomas'. The biblical name Thomas is of Aramaic origin and means 'twin'.

Magnus

Male first name of Scandinavian origin. The name is derived from the Latin *magnus* meaning 'great' as used in the name of the Emperor Carolus Magnus (or Charlemagne) King of the Franks and Holy Roman Emperor in 8th and 9th centuries. Magnus would become the name of seven kings of Norway and would become a common name in the north of Scotland (which was still ruled by Norway until the 15th century).

The most famous Scottish Magnus was the martyred Earl of Orkney, Saint Magnus, for whom the 12th-century Saint Magnus Cathedral in Kirkwall was built. Magnus has remained a popular name in the Northern Isles, and is also known through Magnus Magnusson, the Icelandic presenter of *Mastermind*, who lived in Scotland for most of his life.

Mairead, Maighread, Maisie

Female first names derived from Margaret, meaning 'pearl'. Mairead and Maighread are Scottish Gaelic forms of the name. Maisie is a Scottish diminutive of Mairead and Margaret, and *What Maisie Knew* is a lesser known novel by Henry James.

Mairi, Mhairi

Scottish and Gaelic forms respectively of Mary. The form Mhairi is often pronounced with the 'mh' sounding like a 'v'. The name is especially known from the famous Scottish song 'Mairi's Wedding':

> *Step we gaily on we go*
> *Heel for heel and toe for toe*
> *Arm in arm and row and row*
> *All for Mairi's wedding.*

Malcolm

Scottish male first name and surname that derives from the Gaelic *Mael Coluim* and means 'follower of Saint Columba'. Saint Columba was Scotland's most important religious figure and established Iona as the Christian centre of Scotland in the 6th century. Four of Scotland's kings were called Malcolm, including Malcolm III (also known as Malcolm Canmore), who defeated Macbeth in 1057 and with his wife Queen

Margaret established the royal dynasty that would rule Scotland until the end of the 13th century.

Other famous Malcolms include broadcaster Malcolm Muggeridge, American political activist Malcolm X, Australian Prime Minister Malcolm Fraser, film actor Malcolm McDowell, West Indian cricketer Malcolm Marshall, and the title character of the American television comedy *Malcolm in the Middle*.

Margaret

Greek female first name meaning 'pearl'. Margaret has been a popular first name since the time of Queen Margaret, who reigned with Malcolm III in the 11th century and was known for transforming the Scottish court as well as for her religious piety. She was later canonized as Saint Margaret. St Margaret's Chapel, which is named after her, is the oldest building at Edinburgh Castle – and the oldest surviving building in Edinburgh – dating back to the 12th century.

Margaret the Maid was the short-lived Queen of Scotland whose death at the age of seven in 1290 ended the dynasty founded by Malcolm and Margaret. Margaret Tudor, sister of Henry VIII of England, was married to James IV of Scotland in 1503, and it was their union that would eventually lead to the Union of the Crowns in 1603 through her great-grandson James VI. In 1930, Princess Margaret, the younger sister of the current Queen, was born at Glamis Castle, thus continuing the tradition of Margaret as a royal name.

For centuries Margaret vied with Mary to be the most popular girls' name in Scotland. It became significantly less popular in the late 20th century, however, after Margaret Thatcher became Prime Minister.

Diminutives of Margaret include Maggie, Meg, Marge, Madge, Daisy, and Peggy. Maggie Broon is the glamorous, but fickle, daughter in the cartoon *The Broons* and has been dating numerous different boyfriends over the past 70 years. 'Maggie May' is still the best-known song of singer Rod Stewart.

Marr

Scottish surname that originates from the historic district of Mar in Aberdeenshire. As Mar and Buchan, this district was one the original seven kingdoms of Pictland and would in the 12th century become an earldom of Scotland. The meaning of the place name is unknown, however. The spelling of the surname reflects the Gaelic form of the place name, *Marr*.

Famous Marrs include Scottish political broadcaster Andrew Marr and Johnny Marr, guitarist with The Smiths.

Marshall

Popular surname throughout Britain. The name is derived from the French word *marechal* meaning 'horse servant' and originally was the term for the occupation of farrier or blacksmith. Later it came to mean a person with important duties in a household, and eventually a high official or someone with military responsibilities. The Scots form of the word was *marischal* and the title of Marischal of Scotland, later Earl Marischal, was given to the Keith family from the 12th century. Marischal College in Aberdeen, which would become part of the University of Aberdeen, was founded in 1593.

Martin

Popular male first name and surname that is found throughout Britain and Ireland. The name comes from the Latin name *Martinus*, which in turn is derived from Mars, the Roman god of war. Martin became a popular name from the time of Saint Martin of Tours in the 4th century, and Scotland's first ever church at Whithorn was dedicated to this saint. The name Martin would later also be associated with the original Protestant reformer, Martin Luther. Famous Scottish Martins include the Speaker of the House of Commons, Michael Martin.

Mary

For centuries one of the most popular names for Scottish girls. The name refers to the Virgin Mary, the mother of Jesus, as well as to Mary Magdalene. Mary is the English form of the Latin name *Maria*, which is derived from the Hebrew *Maria* or *Miriam*. The meaning of the name has been the subject of much heated debate, with definitions ranging widely from 'bitter' to 'beloved child' and the more traditionally Christian 'beloved lady'.

Scotland's most famous Marys are missionary Mary Slessor and the unfortunate Mary Stewart, who was at one stage Queen of France and Scotland and heir to the throne of England, but ended up a prisoner for 19 years before being executed in 1587. Although it was probably little comfort to her at the time, Mary's son James would eventually unite the Crowns of England and Scotland for the Stewarts in 1603.

Matheson

Scottish surname with two different origins. In the Highlands, it derives from the Gaelic *Mac Mhathain* meaning 'son of the bear', but in the Lowlands it means 'son of Matthew', with Saint Matthew being the author of the first of the Four Gospels, whose name is derived from the Hebrew *Matt thia* meaning 'gift of God'.

Maxwell

Scottish surname, occasional male first name and prominent Borders family. The name derives from a place in the Borders near Kelso called Maccus Well, named after a 9th-century Saxon noble. Famous Maxwells include renowned Scottish scientist James Clerk Maxwell, who gave the world Maxwell's equations of electromagnetism and is known as 'the father of electronics', author of *Ring of Bright Water* Gavin Maxwell, and a Czech soldier and businessman by the name of Jan Hoch, who would become one of the most famous (and infamous) names in British publishing under his new name of Robert Maxwell.

Melville

Surname that came from members of the Norman family of de Malleville who settled around Edinburgh from the 12th century. The name Malleville is derived from the Norman place name Malleville. It is perhaps not that surprising that people from the town were keen to move to Scotland, as its name means 'bad settlement'. Famous Melvilles include Herman Melville, the author of *Moby Dick*, and his descendant Richard Melville Hall, who is better known as the musician Moby.

Menzies

Scottish surname and occasional male first name. Traditionally, the 'z' is pronounced as 'y'. The Menzies family originated in Perthshire, coming from the Norman family of de Meyners, whose English branch changed the name to Manners. Famous people called Menzies include Australian Prime Minister Robert Menzies, former Scottish chain of newsagents and booksellers John Menzies, and Scottish Liberal Democrat politician Menzies Campbell, whose name is often shortened to 'Ming' Campbell. However, Ming the Merciless from the *Flash Gordon* films has no known connection with the Menzies clan.

Millar, Miller

Surname that has been popular throughout Britain for centuries and takes its name from the occupation of miller. Millar is the Scottish version of Miller, but it is Miller that is actually the more common surname in Scotland. Famous Scottish Millers include Aberdeen footballer Willie Miller and cyclists Robert Millar and David Millar.

Milne

Scottish surname that originated in Aberdeenshire. The name comes from *mylne*, the Scots word for 'mill', and means 'dweller near the mill'. Famous Milnes include the author of *Winnie the Pooh*, A.A. Milne, whose first names were Alan Alexander.

Mitchell

Surname that is found throughout Britain but is especially popular in Scotland. The name either derives from the first name Michael, meaning 'who is like God' (which was brought to Britain through the French variation of *Michel*) or from the Old English word *micel* or Scots word *mickle*, both meaning 'big'.

Famous Scottish Mitchells include James Leslie Mitchell, better known as author of *Sunset Song* Lewis Grassic Gibbon, and the Mitchell Library in Glasgow.

Moir

Scottish surname that originated in the Aberdeen area. The name is a variant of the surname Muir meaning 'moor', and also derives from the Gaelic word *mor* meaning 'big' or 'great'. Famous Moirs include Jim Moir, who is better known as comedian Vic Reeves.

Moira

Scottish female first name. It is the anglicized form of *Maire*, the Irish form of Mary. Famous Moiras include Scottish star of the film *The Red Shoes*, Moira Shearer, and newsreader Moira Stuart.

Moncrieff

Scottish surname that comes from the place called Moncrieff in Perthshire. The name has the same derivation as the town of Crieff, and means 'wooded hill', coming from the Gaelic *monadh* meaning 'hill' and *craoibh* meaning 'trees'.

Montgomery, Montgomerie

Surname that originated from the Norman family of de Montgomery who settled in Ayrshire in the 12th century. The French name came from a village named Montgomery, with *mont* meaning 'mount' and *gomery* deriving from a Viking settler called Gomeric. The place in Wales called Montgomery is named after the same Norman village and family.

Famous Montgomerys with Scottish connections

include L.M. Montgomery, the Canadian author of *Anne of Green Gables*, Montgomery Scott, the Scottish engineer from *Star Trek*, Field Marshal Bernard Montgomery, the victor of El Alamein (known as 'Monty'), golfer Colin Montgomerie, the victor of the European Order of Merit (also known as 'Monty'), and Montgomery Burns, the owner of Springfield's nuclear power plant in *The Simpsons*.

The phrase 'the full Monty' predates the rise to prominence of Colin Montgomerie and sadly does not appear to have any Scottish origins, although Scottish actor Robert Carlyle did play the lead role in the 1997 film of that name.

Morag

Scottish female first name. It derives from the Gaelic name *Mor* meaning 'great' and can also be the Gaelic form of the biblical name Sarah (which means 'princess' in Hebrew). Morag is the name of the lesser-known and smaller monster that is said to reside in Loch Morar.

Morrison

Chiefly Scottish surname meaning 'son of Morris' or 'son of Maurice'. Morris either means 'a follower of the Virgin Mary' or 'dark-skinned' or 'Moorish'.

The Clan Morrison hails from the Isle of Lewis and
is either Irish or Viking in origin. Famous Morrisons
include the supermarket chain Morrisons and singers
Van Morrison and Jim Morrison (who sang with
The Doors and knew the importance in the chilly
Highlands and Islands of lighting fires). American
film star John Wayne was of Scottish descent and was
born Marion Morrison.

Morven, Morvern

Scottish female first names that are often linked
together, but are actually named after two distinct
Scottish places with different meanings. Morven is
the name of separate hills in Aberdeenshire and in
Caithness and probably derives from the Gaelic *mor
bheinn* meaning 'big hill'. Morvern, however, is the
name of a peninsula in Lochaber on the west coast
and comes from the Gaelic *mor bhairne* meaning 'big
gap'. Famous Morverns include the heroine of the
Oban-based book and film *Morvern Callar*.

Muir

Surname that derives from the Scots word for 'moor'.
Famous Muirs include comedy writer Frank Muir
and Scottish environmentalist John Muir, who led
the campaign to establish America's national parks.
The John Muir Country Park was established near

his birthplace of Dunbar.

The word *muir* also appears in many Scottish place names, the most famous of which is perhaps Muirfield in East Lothian, one of the best known golf courses in the world, which has hosted the Open Championship on 15 occasions.

Mungo

Scottish male first name that comes from Saint Mungo, the patron saint of Glasgow. Mungo was in fact the nickname of the 6th-century Saint Kentigern, deriving from the Latin *carissimus amicus* meaning 'dear one', which was first translated into the Brythonic *Myrighu* and then anglicized to Mungo.

Saint Mungo is credited with founding the first church in Glasgow and for performing four miracles with a bird, a tree, a bell, and a fish – objects that would become the four symbols of the city.

Other famous Mungos include Scottish explorer of Africa Mungo Park, pop band Mungo Jerry, who got to number one in 1970 with 'In the Summertime', and Mungo the dog from children's television show *Mary, Mungo & Midge*.

Munro

Scottish surname that became established in Easter Ross. The name comes either from the Irish *rothach* meaning 'man of Ro' (from a place called Roe in the north of Ireland) or from the Gaelic *monadh ruadh* meaning 'red mountain'. In Scotland, the surname is most associated with Hugh Munro who, in 1891, compiled a list of all Scottish mountains of more than 3,000 feet. These peaks were thereafter named Munros in his honour. 'Munro-bagging' is the term given to the pastime of seeking to reach the top of all of Scotland's Munros, which currently number 284.

A variation of the surname Munro is Monroe, a name whose owners include American President James Monroe (who was of Scottish descent) and Hollywood legend Marilyn Monroe.

Murdoch, Murdo

Scottish surname and male first name deriving from the Gaelic *Murchaidh* or *Murchadh* meaning 'sea warrior'. The first name Murdo is an anglicized form of Murdoch. Famous Murdochs include Scottish inventor of gas lighting William Murdoch, novelist Iris Murdoch, and media mogul Rupert Murdoch (whose first name is actually Keith, like his father, whose Australian newspaper business Rupert inherited). No article on this name would be complete without mentioning 'HowlingMad' Murdock from the popular 1980s television show *The A-Team*.

Muriel

Female first name that has been popular in Britain since medieval times. The name is Celtic, but of uncertain origin, possibly being the anglicized form of the Gaelic *Muireall* meaning 'bright sea' (although an Irish origin is more often suggested). Famous Scottish Muriels include author of *The Prime of Miss Jean Brodie,* Muriel Spark, while Muriel Heslop from the Australian film *Muriel's Wedding* is probably of Scottish origin. This film featured the catch-phrase 'You're terrible, Muriel', which has not helped the popularity of the name in recent years.

Murray

Surname and occasional male first name. Murray (also found as Moray) comes from the area of Moray in the north-east of Scotland, which in turn comes from the Gaelic *moraibh* meaning 'sea settlement'.

Famous Murrays include laconic film star Bill Murray, motor racing commentator Murray Walker, Pub Landlord Al Murray, and singer Ruby Murray (who is probably more famous for being rhyming

slang for a curry). Murray is also the name of Australia's second-longest river.

Famous Scottish Murrays include tennis player Andy Murray and businessman David Murray, best known as Chairman of Rangers Football Club. The home of Scottish rugby, Murrayfield in Edinburgh, was named after a local landowner called Andrew Murray.

One of Scotland's most famous comedians was Chic Murray, known for his droll wit. He once said, 'It's a small world, but I wouldn't want to paint it.'

The Clan Murray originated in Moray, but became established in Sutherland and Perthshire, where from the 12th century they became one the important noble families of Scotland. In 1703 they became holders of the title of Duke of Atholl.

Murron

Name of the female character in the 1995 film *Braveheart* who married William Wallace and was then swiftly murdered by the English. In fact, the name of Wallace's wife is believed to have been Marion, but the film's producers thought that audiences would assume that a character with that name would be identified with Maid Marion of the Robin Hood legend. They therefore changed her name to the little-known 'Murron', which either derives from the Irish name *Muireann* meaning 'fair sea' (the name in Celtic mythology of the mother of Fionn mac Cumhaill), or alternatively is an anglicized form of the Gaelic *Muirne* meaning 'dearly beloved'.

Naughtie

Scottish surname that derives from the Aberdeenshire place name of Nochty. The village of Strathdon was formerly known as Invernochty, as it was located where the Water of Nochty met the River Don. The name Nochty does not mean 'badly behaved', but derives from the Gaelic *nochdaidh* meaning 'desolate' or 'bare' in reference to the lack of trees in the area. Famous Naughties include Scottish radio presenter James Naughtie.

Napier

Surname found mainly in Scotland. It is believed to originate from the occupation of naperer, the person in charge of linen in a royal or wealthy household. Famous Scottish Napiers include mathematician John Napier, who invented logarithms in 1614 (presumably in an attempt to better organize the laundry). Napier University in Edinburgh is named after him.

Napier is also a prominent town in New Zealand

which was destroyed by an earthquake in 1931 and rebuilt in the art deco style fashionable at that time.

Neil

First name and surname that derives from the Gaelic and Irish *Niall* and means either 'champion' or 'cloud'. Neil has become a popular name throughout the English-speaking world, and famous Neils include singers Neil Diamond and Neil Young, the first man to step on the moon, Neil Armstrong, Labour leader Neil Kinnock, and Scottish presenter and journalist Andrew Neill.

Neilson

Surname that means 'son of Neil'. Famous Scottish Neilsons include James Neilson, who revolutionized iron production with the invention of a hot-blast oven in 1828.

Nesbitt, Nisbet

Scottish surname that originated in the Borders from several places called Nisbet. The place name is derived from the Old English *nese* meaning 'nose' and *bit* meaning 'piece of ground' and referred to locations that were shaped like a nose. Famous Nesbitts include children's author Edith Nesbit, who wrote *The Railway Children*, Irish actor James Nesbitt, and the hero of the long-running Scottish comedy *Rab C. Nesbitt*, who effectively put an end to the string vest as a popular item of clothing.

Nicol, Nicholl

Scottish male name and surname that was originally a diminutive of Nicholas. Nicholas had long been a popular first name through its association with Saint Nicholas, the patron saint of children, sailors, merchants, and Christmas. It was originally a Greek name meaning 'victory of the people'.

Ninian

Male first name of uncertain, but possibly Welsh, origin. The name is associated with Saint Ninian, who is credited with establishing the first Christian church in Scotland at Whithorn in Galloway in AD397. He later travelled northwards, possibly as far as the Northern Isles, to convert the Picts to Christianity. Ninian gives his name to St Ninian's Isle in Shetland, where an 8th-century hoard of Celtic treasure was discovered in 1958, and also to the Ninian oilfield and pipeline in the North Sea.

Niven

Scottish surname that is a diminutive of the surname MacNiven. It is derived from the Gaelic *naomhain* meaning 'little saint', which comes from *naomh* meaning 'saint'. Nivens were found in Galloway and Ayrshire, and famous Nivens include film star David Niven, who claimed to be born in Kirriemuir in Angus. However, like many of the events chronicled in his two entertaining autobiographies, this was not strictly true. Niven was born and brought up in London and appears never to have set foot in Kirriemuir in his life.

Ogilvie, Ogilvy

Scottish surname that originates from a place in Angus. The name comes from the Brythonic *ugl ma* or *ugl fa* meaning 'high place'. The Ogilvies gained the Scottish title of the Earl of Airlie and are related to the present Queen through the marriage of Angus Ogilvy to her cousin Princess Alexandra. Other famous Ogilvies include Australian golfer Geoff Ogilvy, who won the US Open Championship in 2006.

Oliphant

Surname and clan name. The name came to the Scottish Borders through a Norman surname

Olifard, which was a form of the French first name *Olivier* meaning 'olive tree'. However, there is a separate derivation from the Norse first name *Olaf* meaning 'ancestor's descendant'. The name changed to Oliphant in honour of (incredible as it sounds) the elephant, which was regarded as a symbol of great strength, and the elephant appears on the Clan Oliphant's coat of arms. Famous Oliphants include Scottish songwriter Caroline Oliphant, who wrote traditional Jacobite songs such as 'Charlie Is My Darling'.

Paterson, Patterson

Surname found throughout Britain, and long popular in Scotland. The name means 'son of Patrick'. Patrick derives either from the Latin *Patricius* meaning 'patrician' or 'nobleman' or from the Irish name *Paidric* meaning 'powerful'. Patrick is associated with the patron saint of Ireland, Saint Patrick, and was a popular given name in Scotland until the Reformation.

Famous Scottish Patersons include actor Bill Paterson and financier William Paterson, who founded the Bank of England and was also the man behind the disastrous Darien expedition of 1700 that bankrupted the Scottish economy.

Paton

Scottish surname that derives from Pat, the diminutive of Patrick. Paton is the Scottish form, in comparison with the more common English surname Patton.

Patrick

Male first name that is associated with Saint Patrick, the patron saint of Ireland. The name Patrick is believed to derive from the Latin *Patricius* meaning 'patrician' or 'noble', and was a popular first name in Scotland until the Reformation.

Little is known about the origins of the 5th-century Saint Patrick, he is thought to have been born somewhere on the west coast of the British mainland, possibly in Dunbartonshire. His name occurs in several Scottish place names, including Old Kilpatrick in Dunbartonshire and Portpatrick and Kirkpatrick in Dumfries and Galloway.

Petrie

Surname from the Aberdeen area. It is a diminutive of the male first names Patrick and Peter, with Peter being the anglicized form of the Greek *Petros* meaning 'rock', and Saint Peter being the chief disciple of Jesus and first Bishop of Rome.

Pinkerton

Scottish surname that originated from a place name in East Lothian. The place name is of uncertain derivation, but possibly comes from a Norman family called Pontecardon and ultimately from a place name in France. Famous Pinkertons include Glasgow-born Allan Pinkerton, who founded the Pinkerton National Detective Agency in the United States in 1850.

Pollock

Scottish surname that derives from Pollok, an area of south Glasgow that includes Pollok Country Park, Pollokshields and Pollokshaws. The place name Pollok derives from the Brythonic *poll* meaning 'pool' and *oc* meaning 'little'.

Famous Pollocks include American user of paint Jackson Pollock and South African cricketers Graeme and Shaun Pollock. The surname of 19th-century American President James Knox Polk is a variation of Pollock.

Pringle

Scottish surname that originated in the Borders and comes from the place name of Hoppringle in Roxburgh. The surname has become famous throughout the world due to the knitwear company Pringle of Scotland, founded by Robert Pringle in the Borders in 1815. Pringles is also the name of the highly addictive crisps advertised by that man with the twirly moustache, first sold in America in 1968.

Raeburn

Scottish surname that derives from the place name of Rayburn in Ayrshire. The place name possibly means 'stream where people drink'. Famous Raeburns include Scotland's most famous portrait painter Henry Raeburn, who gave his name to several places in his native Edinburgh, including Raeburn Place, which in 1871 was the location for the first ever rugby international, when Scotland defeated England.

Ramsay

Scottish surname that originated from members of a Norman family called de Ramsey who were given land in Lothian in the 12th century. The family originally took its name from a place near Huntingdon in England called Ramsey, meaning 'ram's island', and Ramsey remains a popular English surname. The Scottish Ramsays would become the Earls of Dalhousie and would build the 15th-century Dalhousie Castle that still stands today. Famous

Scottish Ramsays include chemist and Nobel Prize winner William Ramsay, first British Labour Prime Minister Ramsay MacDonald, and television chef Gordon Ramsay.

Ramsay Street is also one of the most famous streets in Australia, being since 1986 the main location of the soap opera *Neighbours*. The street was named after the Ramsay family, but no Ramsays have lived there for some time, although Ramsay was the previous name of long-running character Madge Bishop.

Rankin

Scottish surname that originated in Ayrshire. The name is derived from *Rand*, a diminutive form of the first name Randolph, which came to Britain from France but is of Germanic origin (with *ran* meaning 'edge' and *wulf* meaning 'wolf'). Famous Rankins include Scottish crime writer Ian Rankin.

Redpath

Surname that originates from the place called Redpath in the Borders. It literally means 'red path'. Scottish Redpaths include painter Anne Redpath and folk singer Jean Redpath.

Reid

Scottish form of the English surname Read or Reed. The name comes from the colour red and usually indicates a red-haired ancestor. It is a very common surname in Scotland either because of or in spite of the large percentage of the population that is naturally ginger.

Famous Scottish Reids have included the brothers William and Jim from The Jesus and Mary Chain, the twin brothers Craig and Charlie from The Proclaimers, and Labour politician and former Home Secretary John Reid (who has yet to record an album).

Rennie

Scottish surname that derives from the French first name *Reynold*, which was brought to Scotland by the Normans. The name *Reynold* has the same origin as the Scandinavian *Rognvaldr*, from which the male first name Ronald is derived, and means 'advisor to the ruler'. Famous Rennies include iconic Scottish architect and artist Charles Rennie Mackintosh.

Renwick

Borders surname that originates from the name of a place in what is now Cumberland in England.

The surname is, however, considered predominantly Scottish. The name Renwick derives from the Old English *hraefn* meaning 'raven' and *wic* meaning 'farm' or 'settlement'. Famous Renwicks include the writer of *One Foot in the Grave*, David Renwick.

Rhona, Rona

Female first name that probably derives from the small Hebridean island of Rona, which lies between Skye and the mainland and has been uninhabited since 1943. The place name is derived from the Norse *Hrauney* meaning 'rough island'. Rhona or Rona is also a diminutive of Catriona. Famous Scottish Rhonas include curler and Olympic gold medallist Rhona Martin and comedian Rhona Cameron.

Ritchie

Surname and male first name that originated in Scotland as a diminutive of Richard. The name Richard was brought to Britain by the Normans and is of Germanic origin with *ric* meaning 'power' and *hard* meaning 'hardy' or 'brave'. Famous Ritchies include film director Guy Ritchie and two contrasting musicians: Ritchie Valens, who sang 'La Bamba', and Ritchie Blackmore, the lead guitarist of rock bands Deep Purple and Rainbow.

Robert

Male first name with Germanic origins, meaning 'bright flame'. Diminutives include Rab, Rabbie, Rob, Robbie, Bob, and Bobby.

The name was brought to Scotland by the Normans, and is especially associated with Scotland through Robert the Bruce and national bard Robert Burns. Robert the Bruce was the first of three Scottish kings called Robert. Other famous Scottish Roberts include outlaw and folk hero Rob Roy Macgregor, the author of *Treasure Island, Dr Jekyll and Mr Hyde,* and *Kidnapped,* Robert Louis Stevenson, actor Robbie Coltrane, Oor Wullie's best friend, Fat Boab, and Edinburgh's most famous Skye terrier, Greyfriars' Bobby. A statue of Greyfriars' Bobby is a popular tourist attraction in Edinburgh, and a Rob Roy is a popular cocktail made from whisky and vermouth.

Robertson

The fifth most common surname in Scotland, meaning 'son of Robert'. Robertsons are found throughout Scotland, but the Clan Robertson originated as an offshoot of the Duncan or Donnachie clan, and the first Robertson chief was named after a Donnachie called Robert who was given land in Perthshire in the 15th century.

Famous Scottish Robertsons include the Robertson family from Paisley, who founded the Robertson's marmalade and jam company, with the Robertson's golliwog being their noted advertising brand.

Ronald

Male first name that is the Scottish variant of the Norse name *Rognvaldr* meaning 'advisor to the ruler'. Diminutives of Ronald include Ron and Ronnie. Famous Ronalds include English film star Ronald Colman, who is best known for fleeing across the Scottish Highlands in Alfred Hitchcock's *The Thirty-Nine Steps*, American president Ronald Reagan, villains Ronnie Biggs and Ronnie Kray, McDonald's clown Ronald McDonald, and *The Two Ronnies* – Ronnie Barker and Scottish comedian Ronnie Corbett.

Rory

Male first name and anglicized version of the Gaelic name *Rhuairdh* or *Ruadhri* meaning 'red king'. Famous Rorys include impressionist Rory Bremner.

Ross

Surname and male first name. The name comes from the region of Ross in the Highlands, ultimately

friday night
with
jonathan
ross

deriving from the Gaelic word *ros* meaning
'headland' or 'promontory' – although there were also
Normans with the surname of de Ros who settled in
the Lowlands.

The Clan Ross dates back to the first Earl of Ross in
13th century. Famous Rosses include singer Diana
Ross, chat-show host Jonathan Ross, Dr Doug Ross,
the character played by George Clooney in *ER*, and
Ross Geller from American comedy *Friends* – who in
one episode does actually play the bagpipes.

Rough

Surname that in Scotland originated in Fife. It
derives from the English word 'rough' or from an old
Scots word *rughe* also meaning 'rough' or 'unkempt'.
Famous Scottish Roughs include goalkeeper Alan
Rough, whose perm at the 1978 World Cup could
certainly be called 'unkempt'.

Roy

Male first name that derives from the Gaelic
ruadh meaning 'red-haired'. Famous Roys include
the Scottish folk hero Rob Roy Macgregor, Irish
footballer Roy Keane, American singer Roy Orbison,
American pop artist Roy Lichtenstein, entertainer
Roy Castle, comic-strip footballer Roy of the Rovers,

and western film star Roy Rogers, who once rode up Princes Street in Edinburgh on his faithful horse Trigger.

The Highland place names Glen Roy, the River Roy, and Roy Bridge all share the same Gaelic origin and similarly mean 'red'.

Russell

Surname and male first name that is popular throughout Britain. The name is derived from the French *rous* and means 'red-haired'. In Scotland the name is found mainly in the Lowlands.

Rutherford

Scottish surname that originates from a place in Roxburgh. The origin of the place name is uncertain, but one suggestion is that it derives from an Old English word *hrythera* meaning 'cattle' combined with the English word 'ford'. Famous Rutherfords include Rutherford Hayes, President of the United States from 1877 to 1881, English film actress Margaret Rutherford, and the first person to split the atom, New Zealand physicist Ernest Rutherford (whose father was Scottish).

Salmond

Surname that is a variation of the name Salmon.
The Salmonds originally come from Perthshire and
famous Scottish Salmonds include First Minister
Alex Salmond. When Salmond and his deputy Nicola
Sturgeon were voted into power in 2007, it was
often remarked that Scotland was now governed by a
couple of fish.

Sandy

Male first name that in Scotland is a diminutive
of Alexander, but can be used as a first name in its
own right. As a female first name, Sandy is usually a
diminutive of Sandra and is not of Scottish origin.
Famous Scottish Sandys include golfer Sandy Lyle.

Scott

Popular Scottish surname and male first name that
means (as you might imagine) 'someone who comes
from Scotland'. The original Scots were in fact
people from Ireland who came to settle in the west of
Scotland from the 5th century onwards and would
eventually give their name to the entire country.
Their name came from the Latin *Scotti* meaning a
not very complimentary 'raiders' or 'pirates'. The
surname Scott became established in the Borders as

a means of differentiating Scots from their English neighbours, and the Scotts became a prominent Border clan and holders of the title of Duke of Buccleuch.

Famous Scotts include the second man to reach the South Pole, Captain Robert Scott, film director Ridley Scott, American ragtime composer Scott Joplin, author of *The Great Gatsby* F. Scott Fitzgerald, film actor George C. Scott, singer Scott Walker of the Walker Brothers, and Chief Engineer Montgomery Scott from *Star Trek*.

The most famous Scottish Scott, however, is novelist Sir Walter Scott, for whom the 200-feet-high tower called the Scott Monument was built in Princes Street Gardens in Edinburgh in 1844. The monument stands next to the Waverley train station that was named after his novel *Waverley*.

Shaw

Surname that is found throughout Scotland, but with different origins. The Shaws of Lowland Scotland take their name from the Old English word *sceaga* meaning 'wood', but in the Highlands, where the Clan Shaw was concentrated at Speyside, the Shaws took their name from the Gaelic first name *Sitheach* meaning 'wolf'. Famous Shaws include Irish playwright George Bernard Shaw.

Shearer

Predominantly Scottish surname that originated from the occupation of sheep-shearer. Famous Shearers include Scottish star of *The Red Shoes*, Moira Shearer, the voice of Mr Burns in *The Simpsons*, Harry Shearer, and footballer Alan Shearer, who presumably comes from a family of Northumbrian, rather than Scottish, sheep-shearers.

Sheena

Popular female first name. It is the anglicized form of the *Sine*, the Gaelic form of Jane, and ultimately comes from the French *Jeanne*, the feminine form of John. Sheena became well known for the Ramones song 'Sheena Is a Punk Rocker', although the name lost popularity after the rise to fame of Scottish singer Sheena Easton (who was not known for her punk output) in the 1980s.

Shona

Popular female first name. It is the anglicized form of *Seonag*, the Gaelic form of Joan and a feminine form of John. Shona can also be the anglicized form of *Seonaid*, the Gaelic form of Janet, which is also a feminine form of John.

Simpson

Surname found throughout Britain but long popular in Scotland. The name means 'son of Simon' (or 'son of Sim' – a diminutive of Simon). In the Bible, Simon was the name of two of Jesus' disciples, and the name derives from the Hebrew *Shimon* meaning 'heard' or 'listening'. Famous Scottish Simpsons include James Simpson, who successfully introduced chloroform as an aid to childbirth.

Sinclair

Surname that derives from a Norman family called St Clair who originated from the French town of that name in Normandy. The St Clairs were given land at Roslin in Midlothian at the end of the 11th century, and it was there that they would build Rosslyn Chapel, famous for its uniquely intricate architecture and connections with the Knights Templar – a place that would many centuries later be featured in the book and film *The Da Vinci Code*. The St Clairs would eventually become the Sinclairs and the family would gain the earldoms of both Caithness and Orkney.

Famous Sinclairs include Henry Sinclair, who is said to have succeeded in sailing to North America and back a century before Columbus, and actor John Gordon Sinclair, who starred as Gregory in the 1981 film *Gregory's Girl* and will always be remembered for teaching Scots the two most important words in the Italian language – *bella* and *bella*.

Skye

Popular female first name that comes from the Isle of Skye. Skye is the largest island in the Inner Hebrides and is known for its beautiful scenery. The Gaelic name for Skye is *An t-Eilean Sgitheanach*, which means 'winged island', and the Norse name for Skye was *Skuyo*, meaning 'island of mist'.

Smilie

Surname found in Lanarkshire. The name is a variation of Smellie, and either derives from an English place called Smalley meaning 'narrow wood' or else a nickname for someone who either smiles or has a particular odour. Scottish television presenter Carol 'Smiley' Smilie presumably takes her name from the former rather than the latter sense.

Smith

The most common surname in Scotland (and the rest of the English-speaking world). The surname derives from the English word 'smith', referring to the occupation of craftsman, as in blacksmith, silversmith, or wordsmith. It is said that the surname became more popular in Scotland after 1746 as people changed their name to this to suppress surnames that might have had Jacobite associations. (Although you might think this would only have raised people's suspicions – much as happens with nervous-looking people called 'Smith' who book hotel rooms.)

Famous Scottish Smiths include economist Adam Smith, the founder of the Boy's Brigade, William Smith, Labour Party leader John Smith, and author Alexander McCall Smith.

Sorley

Scottish male first name. It is the anglicized form of the Gaelic *Somhairle* (Somerled), the name of the 12th-century chieftain who established himself as King of the Isles and through his descendants founded the Clan MacDonald and Clan MacDougall. The name Somerled derives from the Norse *Sumarlior* and means 'summer traveller'. Other famous Sorleys include poet Sorley MacLean.

Stein

Surname that first became established in Scotland in Fife. The name is derived from the male first name

Steven and the surname Stevenson. Famous Scottish Steins include legendary Celtic and Scotland football manager Jock Stein.

Stevenson

Surname found throughout Britain and long popular in Scotland. The name means 'son of Steven', with Steven being a variant spelling of the more traditional Stephen, coming from the Greek *Stephanos* meaning 'crown'. Saint Stephen is known as the first Christian martyr and his feast day takes place on December 26th.

Famous Scottish Stevensons include the remarkable family of six lighthouse engineers, the 'Lighthouse Stevensons', who in the 19th century designed and supervised the construction of the most remote lighthouses around Scotland's coast and islands, saving thousands of lives in the process. The author of *Treasure Island* and *Kidnapped*, Robert Louis Stevenson, was the son of one of these 'Lighthouse Stevensons'.

Stewart, Stuart

Surname and male first name that derives from the English word 'steward'. In Scotland the surname Stewart was given to a Norman noble family called

Fitzalan who were appointed as Hereditary High Stewards of Scotland in the 12th century and given considerable land in Renfrewshire, Atholl, Appin, Balquhidder, and Galloway (where 'Stewartry' remains an alternative name for the former county of Kirkcudbrightshire in recognition of the Stewart influence over the region).

Walter Stewart, the sixth High Steward, would marry Marjorie Bruce, the daughter of Robert I, and Robert II would become the first Stewart monarch in 1371. The Stewarts remained the royal dynasty of Scotland until the death of Queen Anne in 1714. After the accession of James VI to the English crown in 1603, the Stewarts were also the royal family of England.

The royal family of the Stewarts held at one time the dukedoms of Albany, Lennox, and Galloway and the earldoms of Angus, Atholl, Buchan, Carrick, Galloway, Menteith, and Strathearn.

The Royal Stewarts' line of succession came to an end with the overthrow of James VII in 1688 and the death of his daughter Queen Anne in 1714. The Jacobite uprisings of 1715 and 1745 failed to restore the Stewarts to the thrones of England and Scotland, culminating in the final defeat of James VII's grandson Charles Edward Stewart, the Young Pretender, at Culloden in 1746. In 1788 Charles Edward died leaving no heir, which marked the end of the royal dynasty and, unsurprisingly, a decline in the fortunes of the clan.

Famous Stewarts include James IV, Mary, Queen of Scots, James VI, Charles I, Charles II, singer Rod Stewart, motor-racing driver Jackie Stewart, Patrick Stewart, who plays Captain Jean-Luc Picard in *Star Trek: The Next Generation*, American television presenters Martha and Jon Stewart, and legendary film star James Stewart. British film star Stewart Granger's real name was also James Stewart, but he changed it to avoid confusion with his taller American contemporary.

When Mary, Queen of Scots was briefly Queen of France by marriage, she adopted the French spelling of 'Stuart' for her family name. This has remained an alternative spelling for both the surname and first name, and can cause great confusion about whether Mary and Charles, for example, should be Stewarts or Stuarts. In Scotland, Stewart is by far the more popular form of the surname, except on Bute where the Stuarts are a prominent family and built the country house of Mount Stuart. Famous Stuarts include philosopher John Stuart Mill, newsreader Moira Stuart, and *Stuart Little*, the name of a novel and film about a mouse who can talk.

The Royal Stewart tartan is probably the most popular of all the Scottish tartans and is found not only kilts but also on stationery and a plethora of tourist paraphernalia.

Strachan

Scottish surname that originates from a place in Kincardine. The place name is possibly derived from the Gaelic *strath eachain* meaning 'wide valley of the young horse'. Famous Strachans include Scottish footballer and Celtic manager Gordon Strachan.

Struan

Scottish male first name that originated in Perthshire. The name comes from a place called Struan and is associated with the Robertson and Duncan clans. There is also a Struan on Skye, and the name derives from the Gaelic *sruthan* meaning 'small stream'. The name Struan features as the surname of the main family in the novels of American author James Clavell.

Sutherland

Surname and clan name that comes from the former county of Sutherland in the northern Highlands. The name of the county derives from the Norse *Suthr land* meaning 'southern land' as, although the area was at the very north of the Scottish mainland, it was at the very south of the Viking-controlled territory governed for Norway by the Earl or Jarl of Orkney.

Famous Sutherlands include the infamous Elisabeth Sutherland, Countess of Sutherland, under whose name the Sutherland Highland Clearances took place, opera singer Joan Sutherland, and father and son actors Donald and Kiefer Sutherland.

Taggart

Surname that derives from the name MacTaggart and simply means 'priest'. The long-running and internationally popular television series *Taggart* was first shown in 1983 and featured Mark McManus playing Detective Chief Inspector Jim Taggart until the actor's death in 1994. Despite there being no subsequent character with the name, the television series has continued to run as *Taggart*. However, none of McManus's successors have been able to say the phrase 'there's been a murder' with quite the same world-weary Glaswegian relish.

Tavish

Scottish male first name. It is either the anglicized form of *Tamhas*, the Gaelic form of Thomas, or else is derived from the surname MacTavish, which means 'son of Thomas'. Famous Tavishes include Scottish Liberal leader Tavish Scott.

Taylor

Surname that has been popular throughout Britain for centuries and takes its name from the occupation of tailor.

Telford

Surname that originates in Lowland Scotland. It is derived from the surname Telfer, which in turn is derived from the French *taille-fer* meaning 'cut-iron' or 'strong-man'. Famous Scottish Telfords include road, canal, and bridge builder Thomas Telford, after whom Telford College in Edinburgh and the town of Telford in the English Midlands are named.

Tennant, Tennent

Predominantly Scottish surname that derives from the English word 'tenant' meaning 'a farmer who holds land by lease'. It became established in the Lowlands. Famous Tennants include Scottish chemist Charles Tennant, who invented bleaching powder, Scottish actor David Tennant, and Neil Tennant, singer with The Pet Shop Boys.

Tennent's lager is Scotland's best-selling beer. It was

first brewed in 1885 by Hugh Tennent, a member of the Tennent family who founded a brewery in Glasgow in 1740. The firm of Tennent's sponsors and gives its name to Scotland's biggest music festival, *T in the Park*, where the aforementioned lager is readily available to festival-goers.

Thomas

Long established male first name that is popular in Scotland. The name is derived from the Aramaic, meaning 'twin', and was the name of one of the disciples of Jesus in the Bible. The name only became popular in English-speaking countries after the martyrdom of Thomas Becket in the 12th century. Diminutives of Thomas include Tom, Tommy, Tam, and Tosh. Famous Scottish Thomases include film star Thomas Connery, better known throughout the world as Sean.

The most famous Scottish Thomas, however, is the hero of the 1791 epic poem by Robert Burns called *Tam o' Shanter*. This is often considered Burns' best poem and it gave the world not only the term 'cutty-sark' (which refers to the somewhat revealing shirt worn by an attractive female witch), but also Tam o' Shanter himself, who gave his name to a popular bonnet that was traditionally blue and had a pompom.

Thomson

The fourth most common surname in Scotland.
It means 'son of Thomas' and is also the anglicized
form of MacTavish and Macintosh. Famous Scottish
Thomsons include architect Alexander 'Greek'
Thomson, the Dundee newspaper and comics firm
of D.C. Thomson, which gave the world *The Beano,
The Dandy*, *The Broons*, and *Oor Wullie*, and Bobby
Thomson, the Glasgow-born American who hit the
winning home run in the 1951 National League
baseball championship, one of the most dramatic
moments in baseball history and known as 'the shot
heard round the world'.

The spelling 'Thomson' is generally seen as the
Scottish form of the name, in comparison with the
English spelling 'Thompson'.

Another Scottish variant of the name is Tamson. This
form is best known from the saying 'We're a' Jock
Tamson's bairns', which means that we are all alike
never mind where we come from.

Thorburn

Scottish surname from the Lowlands. It derives
from an Old English first name *Thurbjorn*, which
is Norse in origin, with *Thur* deriving from Thor,
the Norse god of war, and *bjorn* meaning 'bear' or

'warrior'. Famous Thorburns include Canadian Cliff Thorburn, winner of the 1980 World Snooker Championship.

Urquhart

Scottish surname that takes its name from a place in Inverness-shire. The name is famous from the now ruined 13th-century Urquhart Castle on the shores of the Loch Ness, which is (according to tourist guides) a good place to see the Loch Ness Monster. The name Urquhart is believed to be of Pictish or Brythonic origin with *air* meaning 'on' or 'upon' and *cardden* meaning 'thicket' or 'wood', thereby making Urquhart mean 'woodside'.

Famous Urquharts include Francis Urquhart, the fictional Prime Minister played by Ian Richardson in the television series *House of Cards*, who when asked if he was Scottish replied, 'You might very well think that, but I couldn't possibly comment.'

Vaila

Female first name that is popular in Shetland. It comes from the island of Vaila, west of the Mainland of Shetland, which had at the last census a population of only two. The island's name comes from the Norse name *Valey*, which is of uncertain origin. The ending *ey* means 'island', and it has been suggested that the name might mean 'island of peace', although it is probably more likely that *Val* derives from a Norse first name.

Walker

Surname that has long been popular in Scotland as well as the rest of Britain. It originates from the medieval occupation of walking or 'waulking' on woollen cloth to thicken the fibres. Famous Scottish Walkers include the Kilmarnock whisky producers Johnnie Walker and the Speyside food manufacturers Walkers Shortbread.

Wallace

Surname that is believed to denote someone of Welsh ancestry. The ancestors of the Wallaces may alternatively have come from the ancient kingdom of Strathclyde, whose inhabitants were Britons and spoke a language closer to Welsh than Gaelic. The Wallaces were concentrated in Ayrshire and included Scotland's national hero, William Wallace (although there has been much dispute about where William Wallace actually came from).

The Wallace Monument near Stirling is a 220-feet-high tower built in 1869 to commemorate

Wallace as a representation of Scotland's national identity. The location was chosen to be close to Wallace's most famous victory at Stirling Bridge in 1297.

Other famous Wallaces include Lew Wallace, the author of *Ben Hur*, and inventor and cheese-lover Wallace, who along with Gromit has starred in *The Wrong Trousers* and *The Curse of the Were-Rabbit*.

Watson

One of Scotland's most popular surnames, also found throughout Britain. The name means 'son of Walter' or, more particularly, 'son of Wat' – Wat and Watt being diminutives of Walter. The given name Walter was brought to Britain by the Normans, but is Germanic in origin and derives from *wald* meaning 'rule' and *heri* meaning 'army'. Famous Scottish Watsons include radar pioneer Robert Watson-Watt. Also deserving of a mention is Doctor John Watson, the companion of Sherlock Holmes, who although not Scottish himself was created by the Scottish author Arthur Conan Doyle.

Watt

Surname that is particularly associated with the north-east of Scotland. The name is derived from

Wat or Watt, the shortened forms of the popular first name Walter. The name Walter is of Germanic origin and combines the words *wald* meaning 'rule' and *heri* meaning 'army'. Famous Scottish Watts include radar pioneer Robert Watson-Watt and the inventor of the steam engine, James Watt, who is commemorated in Edinburgh's Heriot-Watt University. James Watt would also give his name to the watt as in the internationally accepted unit of power, with a kilowatt being a thousand watts, a megawatt being a million watts, a gigawatt being one billion watts, and a terawatt being one trillion watts (which would certainly keep a lot of light bulbs going).

Weir

Surname that is common in Scotland. The name does not refer to a dam-like structure, but originates from the Norman family of Vere. The Veres came from the town of Vere in Normandy and acquired land in Lanarkshire. Famous Weirs include Australian film director Peter Weir, Scottish actress and writer Molly Weir, and her naturalist and broadcaster brother Tom Weir, whose show *Weir's Way* was shown on Scottish television at three o'clock in the morning for over 20 years.

The Renfrewshire town of Bridge of Weir is, however, named after the English word 'weir', with the weir in question crossing the River Gryffe, near to where the bridge was originally built.

Wendy

Female first name. If Wendy is not technically a Scottish name, it was first made popular by Scottish author J.M. Barrie in 1904 in the play *Peter Pan*. The name of the character Wendy Darling, who goes to Neverland in the play, arose after the young daughter of one of Barrie's friends called the writer 'my friendy-wendy'. Famous Scottish Wendys include short-lived Labour leader Wendy Alexander.

Wilkie

Scottish surname that originated in Lothian and is a diminutive of William. Famous Wilkies include the author of *The Woman in White*, Wilkie Collins, and two Scottish David Wilkies: the 19th-century painter and the 1976 Olympic swimming gold medallist.

William

Male first name of Germanic origin. The name comes from the Germanic *Wilhelm*, with *wil* meaning 'will' or 'resolution' and *helm* meaning 'helmet' or 'protection'. It was brought to Scotland in its current spelling form by the Normans. William I was king of Scotland from 1165 to 1214. He was given the nickname 'the Lion' and is believed to have introduced the Lion Rampant as the royal standard of Scotland.

The name is also associated with the Protestant Dutchman William of Orange who, with his Stewart wife Mary, became King and Queen of England and Scotland in 1688, overthrowing the reigning Catholic monarch James VII, who also happened to be Mary's father. William is affectionately known as 'King Billy' by certain sectors of Scottish society, although he never ever set foot in Scotland. The Highland town of Fort William was originally named after him.

Diminutives of William include Bill, Billy, Willie, and Wullie. Famous Scottish Williams include William Fisher, the Church of Scotland elder who was the target for Robert Burns' satire 'Holy Willie's Prayer', William McGonagall, who gained the reputation of being the world's worst poet, comedian and actor Billy Connolly, rugby commentator Bill McLaren, and comic character Oor Wullie, who has been entertaining readers with his dungarees and bucket since 1936.

Another William who was popular with Scottish children was 'Wee Willie Winkie', who featured in a Scottish nursery rhyme by William Miller with these lines:

Wee Willie Winkie rins throu the toun
Up stairs and doon stairs in his nicht goon
Tirlin at the window, cryin at the lock
Are the weans in their bed, for its noo ten o clock.

This sounds like a precursor of today's experiment of enforcing curfews on young people in our towns and cities.

Arguably even more famous than Oor Wullie and Wee Willie is Scotland's greatest patriot and star of *Braveheart*, William Wallace, who led the Scottish resistance in the Wars of Independence until his execution in 1306.

And even more famous than William Wallace and Oor Wullie (according to a recent poll to find the best known Scotsman in the world) is Groundskeeper Willie from *The Simpsons*.

Wilson

Third most common surname in Scotland, and a popular surname throughout Britain. The name means 'son of William'. Famous Scottish Wilsons include former world darts champion Jocky Wilson and *One Foot in the Grave* star Richard Wilson, who simply does not believe that his name is so common.

The surname Williamson has the same meaning and is also a common surname in Scotland.

Wishart

Surname from the north-east of Scotland. It comes from the Norman name *Guishard* meaning 'prudent'. George Wishart was an early Scottish Protestant reformer who was burned at the stake in 1546.

Witherspoon

Surname of Scottish origin. The name comes from the English words *wether* (or its Scots equivalent *wedder*) meaning 'sheep' and *spong* meaning 'pasture'. Famous Witherspoons include Scottish minister John Witherspoon, who signed the American Declaration of Independence, and his descendant the film actress Reese Witherspoon. The surname Wetherspoon has become well known as the name of a chain of pubs, but does not appear to have a Scottish origin – although the pubs are certainly popular with Scots.

Young

Popular surname throughout Britain. The name originates from the English word 'young' and was used as a surname to differentiate fathers and sons who had the same first name. Famous Scottish Youngs include chemist and paraffin pioneer James

Young, brothers Angus and Malcolm Young from Australian rock band AC/DC (who were both born in Glasgow), and *Desert Island Discs* presenter Kirsty Young.

Suggestions for Further Reading

The Scottish Islands: Hamish Haswell-Smith (Canongate)

Tracing Your Scottish Ancestors: Cecil Sinclair (Mercat Press)

Oxford Dictionary of First Names: Patrick Hanks & Flavia Hodges (OUP)

Scottish Place Names: WFH Nicolaisen (Batsford)

Scottish Place Names: David Ross (Birlinn)

Scottish Surnames: George Mackay (Lomond Books)

Bumper Book Of Babies Names: Jacqueline Harrod & Andre Page (Clarion)

Collins Guide to Scots Kith & Kin (Harper Collins)

Scottish Surnames: David Dorward (Mercat Press)

Scotland's Place Names: David Dorward (Mercat Press)

Clans & Tartans: James MacKay (Lomond Books)

Scottish First Names: George MacKay (Lomond Books)

Scottish Christian Names: Leslie Alan Dunkling (Johnson & Bacon)

Illustrated Encyclopedia of Scotland: edited Iseabail MacLeod (Lomond Books)

Collins Encyclopedia of Scotland: John & Julia Keay (Harper Collins)

Surnames of Scotland: George F. Black (Birlinn)

Scottish Place Names (Harper Collins)

Scottish Words (Harper Collins)